THE MIGHTY MAGPIE BOOK!

Collins
Glasgow & London

First published in this edition 1977
Published by William Collins Sons and Company Limited
Glasgow and London
© 1977 Thames Television

Printed in Great Britain

ISBN 0 00 103354 9 (paperback)
0 00 103383 2 (cased)

Filmset by SX Composing Limited
61 Oakwood Avenue
Leigh-on-Sea, Essex

CREDITS

The Magpie Team
Producer Tim Jones. **Associate Producer** Lesley Burgess.
Directors Neville Green, Audrey Starrett, Stan Woodward,
Peter Yolland. **Researchers** Mary Austin, Helen Best,
Ted Clisby, Helen Dickinson, Kate Marlow, Gill Southcott.
Production Assistants Michele Green, Pat Leslie,
Pat MacLaurin. **Film Editors** Terry Harris, John Plummer.
Assistant Film Editors Bernie Cooper, Chris Thompson.
Secretary Jean Lyall. **Correspondence Girls** Pat Wise,
Marion Howells, Marita Samuels

The Editorial Team
Editors: Vivien Bowler and Vicki Webster
Designer and illustrator: Helen Lindon

Photographs and Illustrations
Thames Television wish to thank the following photographers,
organisations and artists who have supplied photographs and
illustrations for this book.

Photographs and illustrations have been credited by page
number. Where more than one photograph appears on the
page, references are made in the order of the columns
across the page and then from top to bottom.

Cover: Helen Lindon. 6–8: Brian Moore. 14: Popperphoto,
Popperphoto, Popperphoto. 17: Thames. 18–23: Gerry
Embleton. 28–31: Peter Brannon. 32: Thames. 34–39: Jean
Flynn. 40–41: EMI. 42: Science Museum. 43: John Sanders.
44: John Sanders. 45: John Sanders. 49: Walt Disney
Productions. 50–51: Walt Disney Productions. 52: Walt
Disney Productions. 53–56: Thames. 57: RNLI. 58: RNLI.
59: Roger Jones/Esso, The Observer. 60: The Observer.
61: Pat Morris. 62–63: (colour artwork) George Downes.
63: (line) George Downes, (photo) Pat Morris. 64: Pat
Morris (photo), Marion Mills (line). 65: Neil Hyde. 70:
Museum Ferdinandeum, Innsbruck, RAF Museum. 71:
Smithsonian Institution. 74: John Salisse, John Salisse.
72–73: Camera Press, Frank Lindon (artwork). 82: Pat
Morris, Thames, Pat Morris, Pat Morris. 83: Thames, Pat
Morris, Pat Morris, Pat Morris. 84–88: Satour. 86–87: Satour.
90: Mike Roberts. 91: Mike Roberts, Mike Roberts, Mike
Roberts, Mike Roberts. 92: Mike Roberts, Mike Roberts. 93:
Pat Morris, Thames. 94–95: Pat Morris, Pat Morris, Pat
Morris, Pat Morris, Pat Morris, Pat Morris. 96: Pat Morris.
102–103: NME. 106: National Motor Museum, Beaulieu,
Museum of London. 107: Castle Museum York, Gladstone
Pottery Museum. 109: Brian Moore. 113: Frank Lindon
(model Rachel Morris). 114: Pat Morris, Pat Morris, Pat
Morris, Pat Morris, Pat Morris, Pat Morris. 115: Peter
Kestervan. 116: Pat Morris. 117–119: Thames. 120–125:
Jane B Johnstone. 127: Thames.

A Word

STAND BY STUDIO, ONE MINUTE . . . Well
this is it, another programme, hope it's going
to work—tricky rehearsal today . . . *FORTY-FIVE
SECONDS STUDIO, LET'S SETTLE DOWN
NOW* . . . Hope the tiger doesn't bite anyone . . .
STOP TALKING NOW STUDIO . . . 'Where is
Jenny? . . . Well get her in shot' . . . *THIRTY
SECONDS STUDIO* . . . 'Get Mick in. What?
I don't believe it. Get him off the 'phone' . . .
TWENTY SECONDS STUDIO . . . 'Good Luck
everyone' . . . *STAND BY TELECINE* . . . *TEN,
NINE, EIGHT* . . . starting to sweat a bit now . . .
SEVEN, SIX . . . 'Roll Film' . . . *FIVE, FOUR,
THREE, TWO, ONE* . . . 'Take Film' . . . *ON AIR
STUDIO* . . . One for sorrow, Two for joy,
Three for a girl, Four for a boy . . . 'Stand by
Studio, coming to you' . . . Five for silver,
Six for gold, Seven for a secret never to be
told, *M-A-G-P-I-E.*

Hello and welcome to the Mighty Magpie
Book. As you can see it's a rather different book
than you are used to . . . Notice that I have
called it a book, because that is what it is. It
may be a little smaller in size but it has many
more pages and you will see as you read on,
that really it isn't small at all—it is bigger and
better than before.
Magpie started in 1968. I wonder how many
of you can remember back that far . . . Man was

from the Producer

trying, but hadn't yet landed on the moon, Princess Anne was still at school, and you would have bought your sweets in Pounds, shillings and pence. If you had heard of 10p you would have said it was part of a packet of Frozen Peas.

Since 1968 a lot of Magpie programmes have been made—actually there have been about 750. In those programmes we have shown you enough films to stretch from London to Birmingham. What we have always tried to do on the programme, as well as in the Magpie Book, is to show anything which we think will interest all of you at least some of the time. Many of the exciting things we do are suggested by you, the viewers, which is why your letters are so important to us. For example, if we do an exciting item about Motor Cross, one of you is bound to write in and suggest, say, Motor Cycle Scrambling. As well as the exciting things we do on Magpie, we try also to show you in a fun way, for example, how to cook or how to furnish your own room. You can also be very proud of what you have all done to save the lives of animals who are in danger, through watching our series on Endangered Species. Also, even more important, are the many children who are handicapped who have been helped over the years through our successful Magpie Appeals. There are many things that are wrong with the world and all of us hope in our own small way to try to help put things right.

But what is Magpie? Is it the presenters? No, not really, although they indeed are a very important part of the programme. No, Magpie is really your programme. We try as a team to show you things which we hope will entertain you and at the same time tell you a little about the world around you. To do this, each year we go off on our holidays to a foreign land. We try to choose places which quite often you might not be able to visit. In the films we make abroad we try to show you how the children of other countries live—and you know, it is amazing how alike children are all over the world. They may speak a different language but they watch quite often the same television programmes as you do. They may live in the desert but they go to school in a tent and, just as you do, moan and groan about the lessons they have to learn. One of the things that television has done since 1968 when Magpie first started, is to bring all the nations of the world closer together, because with the help of communication satellites in the sky, we can link up with nearly everywhere in the world. Of course, it would be difficult to do a live programme and transmit it all over the world—because while we are awake in Britain, people will be asleep in America and just going to bed in Australia. So you see, it would be a little difficult, but I hope one day to be able to do a Magpie which would bring together in one programme, children from all over the world.

And now, having told you a little of what Magpie is all about, let us take a look at your smashing new Magpie Book. Because it is smaller, this means that it can be put easily into a school satchel, or hidden in a desk at school (don't tell teacher). If you are travelling with your Mums and Dads in the car or train, you will find plenty of competitions and quizzes to pass the time. Also many stories and things to keep you happy on cold winter evenings. There are also many things to create in our Make and Do sections . . . In fact there are so many goodies I can't wait to read on.

Well, enough of me. Thanks to my smashing team for making the programmes and to you for watching and sending in your ideas. Now read on and, if you like it, tell your friends.

Bill Jones

CONTENTS

Smitten by Magpie Madness miss 2 goes

Taken prisoner throw 6 to get out

Bike tyre punctured go back 3 spaces

Forgot to put film in camera back 2 spaces

Marooned miss 2 turns until lifeboat rescues you

Caught in blizzard wait 3 turns

Too much ginger beer throw a 3 to clear hiccups.

HIC!

HIC!

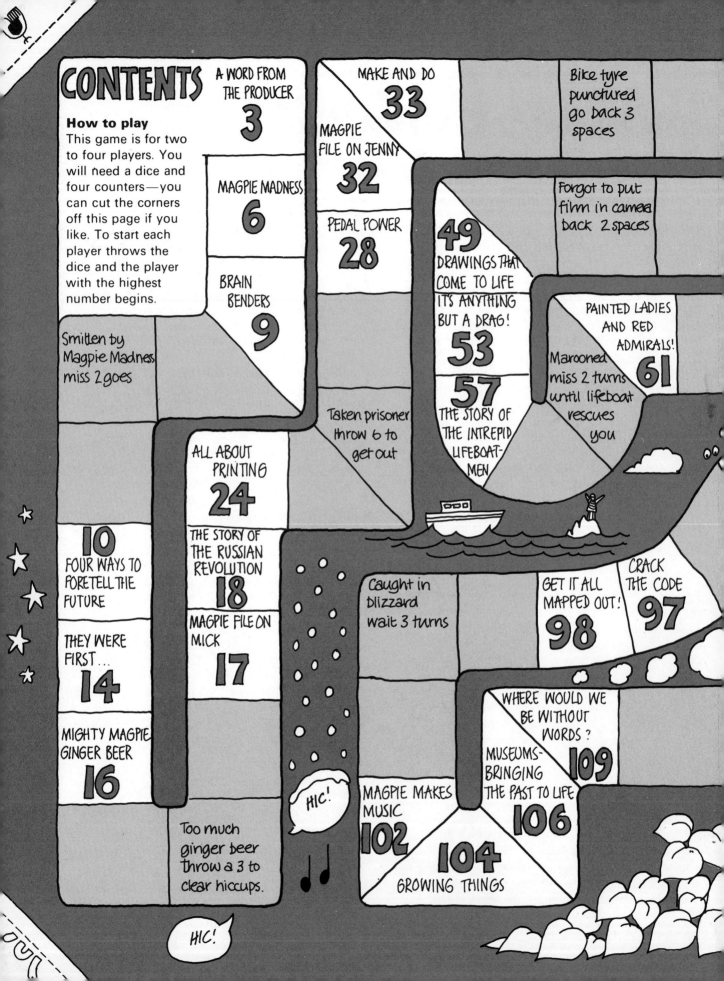

Magpie Madness

by Martyn Day

What's in a name?

The zoological name for the Magpie is *Pica pica*, and the bird is noted for its noisy chatter and its pilfering habits! The old country name for Magpie is 'Maggot-Pie', a mixture of 'Margaret' and 'Pied', meaning Black and White. In olden days Bishops were often called Magpies because they wore black and white robes, and in target shooting, the score made by hitting the outermost ring but one on the target is called a Magpie because it was usual to wave black and white flags when this ring was hit.

Left, right

Including Jenny and Mick, there are 25 people working on the Magpie production team. Of these, three are left handed—an unusual figure as the national average is one person in 20. The proportion of left handed people has decreased since Stone Age times, when there were equal numbers of left-handed and right-handed people.

It is thought that this decline was brought about by the custom of carrying a shield in the left hand, to protect the heart, and the sword in the right hand. Some very famous left handed people include Julius Caesar, Michelangelo, Jack the Ripper, Paul McCartney, Julie Andrews, Rod Steiger, and Charlie Chaplin.

Right type?
In the Magpie offices 12 typewriters are used for writing the scripts and answering your letters. Each typewriter has an inky ribbon that is renewed about three times a year. As each ribbon is 10 metres long, it means that 360 metres are used in the office each year, enough to wrap around Mick's head over 540 times! Typecast for the job, perhaps?

How long?
Magpie started in July 1968. If all the programmes made since then were stuck together they would run for 18,522 minutes . . .which means that to see them all you would have to sit up for nearly 13 days, *and* nights! Also, since 1968 the three Magpie correspondence girls, Pat, Marion and Marita have answered over 328,500 letters . . . (a collection of 63,729,000 words), that would make a pile over 26 metres tall. Imagine the amount of lick needed for all those stamps!

Stars' stars
Jenny is a Leo which means that she is extrovert, with a natural sense of humour. Because of her ruling Sun, she likes flamboyant and stylish clothes, with a preference for gold jewellery. Leos like to be in charge of the situation, and can be obstinate, but generally they are warm hearted and generous . . . just like Jenny!

Mick is an Aquarius, the sign of the genius, and the eccentric! Although it takes time to get to know an Aquarian, they are very sociable people, and like mixing with crowds. They are often unconventional, with a taste for the unusual, and their ruling sign, Uranus, gives them the ability to cope with sudden change, a most useful asset in this rapidly changing world!

Present, correct

During the course of each programme, Mick and Jenny each breathe 168 litres of air. Each breath contains over 300 million molecules that have been used before by someone else, perhaps by Shakespeare, Joan of Arc or even Starsky and Hutch!

More stars

Do you fancy seeing some of those 1968 Magpies again? Well, if you travelled to the star, Sirius A (Alpha Canis Majoris), or the Dog Star as it is called, with a powerful TV receiver, you would be there in time to receive the TV signals that transmitted 'Magpie' way back in 1968. Radio and TV waves travel at approximately 186,000 miles a *second*, but Sirius A is so far away from Earth that it takes nearly nine years for these signals to reach its surface! Have a look for Sirius A tonight. It is visible in winter time, and it is the brightest star in the sky! Perhaps the Sirians are watching a new children's programme tonight!

Miles of viewers

Every week about 8 million people watch Magpie. If all these people were to form a queue outside the Magpie studio in Teddington, it would be 1,600 miles long! If these people were then invited into the studio, it would take them 185 days and nights to pass through the door!

BRAIN BENDERS

1 DAVID IS THREE YEARS YOUNGER THAN PAUL. BUT IN SIX YEARS TIME PAUL WILL BE TWICE AS OLD AS DAVID IS NOW. HOW OLD ARE THE TWO BOYS?

2 CAN YOU MAKE TWO TRIANGLES FROM 5 MATCHSTICKS?

3 CAN YOU SEE HOW TO HOLD A PIECE OF STRING ONE END IN EACH HAND AND TIE A KNOT IN THE STRING WITHOUT LETTING GO OF EITHER END?

4 DRAW THE TRIANGLES IN ONE CONTINUOUS LINE WITHOUT CROSSING ANY LINES OR TAKING THE PENCIL OFF THE PAPER.

NOW TRY THIS. YOU CAN GO OVER THE SAME LINES AS OFTEN AS YOU LIKE. DRAW THE FIGURE IN ONE CONTINUOUS LINE, MAKING THE FEWEST POSSIBLE NUMBER OF TURNS. CAN YOU DO BETTER THAN TEN TURNS?

5 WHICH IS HEAVIER, A POUND OF FEATHERS OR A POUND OF LEAD?

6 A TRICK FOR GUESSING NUMBERS. GET A FRIEND TO CHOOSE TWO NUMBERS, FROM ONE TO NINE, DOUBLE ONE OF THE NUMBERS, ADD FOUR, MULTIPLY BY FIVE AND ADD THE OTHER NUMBER. WHEN YOU GET THE RESULT, MENTALLY TAKE AWAY TWENTY AND THAT THEN GIVES YOU A TWO FIGURE NUMBER. THE TWO NUMBERS ARE THE NUMBERS THAT YOUR FRIEND THOUGHT OF.

7 CAN YOU FILL IN THE BLANKS WITH ONE OF THESE NUMBERS 1, 2, 3, 4, 5, 6, 7, 8, 9 SO THAT EACH SIDE ADDS UP TO 20? HINT: THE THREE CORNER NUMBERS MUST ADD UP TO 15.

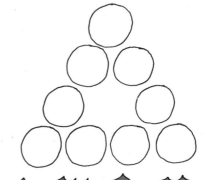

ANSWERS ON PAGE 128

WHAT NEXT?
-FOUR WAYS TO FORETELL THE FUTURE
by Mick Loftus

Aries, the Ram,
21 March—20 April

Taurus, the Bull,
21 April—20 May

Gemini, the Twins,
21 May—20 June

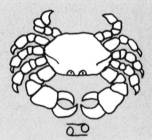

Cancer, the Crab,
21 June—20 July

Can the future be predicted? It's a question that has fascinated man down the ages since he discovered that dark clouds were a warning of rain. Early fortune-tellers claimed they could tell the future from the insides of birds and animals, cut out and spread on the ground. According to various schools of thought, your future can be read in the stars, in the playing cards, in the palm of your hand, in the bumps on your head, in the dreams you dream—and even in the tea-leaves which are left in your cup! Many books have been written about all these methods. But to get you started, here's a brief look at four of the best-known ones.

Astrology
History tells us that man has looked to the stars to foretell the future for at least 2,500 years. The word 'astrology' comes from the Greek *astron*, a star, and *logos*, a discussion, so it means literally 'a conversation with the stars'.

Astrologers (not to be confused with **astronomers,** whose interest in the stars is purely scientific) observe the heavens and take note of the changing positions of the moon and the planets in relation to the sun, believing that their movements govern all that happens in the world. From their findings they can plot the future course of any person's life. To do this accurately, they need to know not only the date and place of a person's birth, but also the exact time of day he or she was born. Only then can they make meaningful predictions for an individual's life. The word 'horoscope' means 'a consideration of the hour' so it's easy to see why the daily 'stars' forecasts in the newspapers are often incorrect—they're much too general to be correct for everyone.

These popular horoscopes are based on the twelve signs of the zodiac, the imaginary circle made by the sun as the earth revolves around it. Each sign represents a different constellation of stars and covers a period of a month. The drawings above show you the symbols used for each sign and the month they apply to, so it's easy enough to see which sign you were born under. But the astrologer will also take into account the planets which were in your part of the circle when you were born, because each planet says something different about your future life. The Moon means *change*, Venus *peace*, Mercury *activity*, the Sun *vitality*, Mars *energy*, Jupiter *riches*, Saturn *poverty*, Uranus *disruption* and Neptune *chaos*!

Obviously, accurate forecasting is a job for the professionals (some Indian universities still offer degrees in astrology) but many amateurs have dabbled in star-gazing with outstanding success.

Leo, the Lion,
21 July—21 August

Virgo, the Maiden,
22 August—22 September

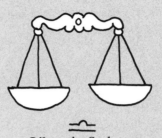

Libra, the Scales,
23 September—22 October

Scorpio, the Scorpion,
23 October—22 November

Sagittarius, the Archer,
23 November—20 December

Capricorn, the Goat,
21 December—19 January

Aquarius, the Water-Carrier,
20 January—18 February

Pisces, the Fish,
19 February—20 March

Cartomancy

This is the name given to the art of reading the future from a series of playing cards selected at random by the person whose fortune is to be told (the subject). It's a lot easier than astrology because it doesn't call for a lot of expert knowledge. All you need is an ordinary pack of playing cards and a book to give you the meaning of each card.

To begin with, all the twos, threes, fours, fives and sixes are removed from the pack. Then the subject shuffles the remaining 32 cards and deals them face upwards in four rows of eight, left to right, working downwards. If the subject is male, he is represented by one of the Kings: of diamonds if he is fair-haired and blue-eyed; of hearts if fair-haired and brown-eyed; of clubs if brown-haired and brown-eyed; and of spades if black-haired and brown-eyed. If female, the subject selects a Queen to represent her on the same basis.

The cards surrounding the subject's selected card in the layout must be read very carefully, as they indicate the immediate future. So must the ninth card from the subject's card, counted in either direction. A further reading can be taken by counting every ninth card starting from the top left. And finally by reading the combined meanings of the first and 32nd cards, the second and 31st cards, and so on to the 16th and 17th.

The cards can have many different meanings (which is why they must be read carefully) but here are a few for you to try:

Diamonds: Seven means a gift, jewellery or children; Eight, road travel, short journey; Nine, sudden events, wounds, quarrels; Ten, town, city, or success; Jack, a selfish, bad-tempered person; Ace, money, a ring or a letter.

Clubs: Seven, success or victory; Eight, a firm friend, agreement; Nine, fun, pleasure and company; Ten, a long journey overland, success by overcoming obstacles; Jack, a real friend who'll look after you; Ace, good luck and success.

Hearts: Seven, a small wish, domestic changes; Eight, clothes, invitations, love, furniture; Nine, joy, a wish granted; Ten, marriage, success, a change for the better; Jack, your dearest friend or closest relation; Ace, good luck, a cot or cradle.

Spades: Seven, an upset or removal; Eight, sickness, loss, a quarrel; Nine, disappointment, delay, failure; Ten, far-off things, a long sea voyage; Jack, a friend who might help you, but needs a push; Ace, a job or position.

Palmistry

Ask a gipsy what the future has in store for you, and he'll almost certainly reply that you have it in the palm of your hand. No two hands are the same, and the art of palmistry is to reveal what the different shapes and markings mean.

Palmistry begins with the study of the different types of hand. This is known as Cheirognomy, and its purpose is to discover what kind of person the hand belongs to. For example, long, tapering fingers with smooth, arched nails are associated with people of good taste and refinement, lovers of music, brightness and beauty. People with large, broad hands and square finger-tips are usually more down to earth, sticklers for neatness, punctuality and correctness. And big, muscular hands which spread like spades at the finger-tips indicate an ambitious, practical, hard-working person not easily put off by obstacles. These are the three most usual types of hand, but there are many more, including combinations of these three.

Having assessed the subject's character in this way, the palmist will then proceed to study the lines of the hand's palm. This is known as Cheiromancy, the art of determining the future of the hand's owner.

Not all hands have the same kind of lines in the same positions, but a look at the diagram (and at your own hand by comparison) will help you identify them. Here's what they mean:

The Life Line, when clear-cut and not crossed by other lines, indicates good health and long life. But don't worry if yours is short or faint—the other lines affect health and long life, too!

The Heart Line shows your affections and emotions. The stronger and longer the line, the more you will attract friends.

The Head Line: if it's long and strong you have good mental abilities, if it's short you're more likely to be better at practical things.

The Fate Line should be long, clear and unbroken for a fortunate life. Where it fades or breaks, bad luck is likely.

The Health Line shows good health when it's clear and unbroken. But don't despair if you haven't got one! It means you'll probably be healthy provided the Life Line is clear and long.

The Girdle of Venus is most often found in the hands of sensitive people, poets, worriers, restless spirits.

The Line of Fortune indicates success when it's clear, deep and straight, especially in the fields of art, literature and science.

The Marriage Line, when clear and unbroken, means lasting attachment to your partner. When broken it suggests the end of a partnership. If you have more than one line here—that's the number of times you will marry!

The Bracelet is another indication of a long and useful life, when it's clearly marked.

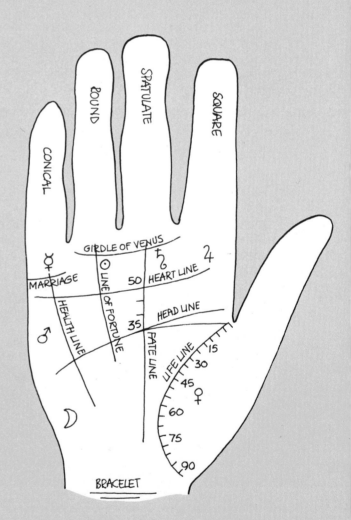

Dream Analysis

This is probably the least precise of all the popular methods of foretelling the future—but it can be fun! All you have to do is keep a notebook beside the bed and write down what you dreamed about as soon as you wake up. Then check them against this list:

If you dream about:	It could mean:
An accident	If it happened to you, great success. If to someone else, you have enemies.
Animals	If pets, the return of absent friends. If wild, expect trouble from enemies.
Bells	If you heard them, expect good news.
A bridge	Crossing over it: good luck. Passing under it: bad luck.
A castle	If in one, you'll inherit money. If it's distant, you won't.
Climbing	Some honour is in store for you.
Dancing	Good news on the way.
Drowning	Whether you or someone else, a good sign.
Eating	A quarrel with friends.
An elephant	You'll be rich one day.
Fighting	If you win, look out for trouble. If you lose, your worries will fade.
Fire	Good health and happiness.
Games	If playing them, good news is coming.
A garden	Good luck for you or your family.
Horses	If riding, you'll marry into money. If falling off, expect bad luck.
Ice	Your sweetheart is kind and true. If skating, beware of people's demands.
Jewels	If yours, happiness lies ahead.
Kissing	Good luck, especially if against someone's will.
Lemons	Family quarrels will try your patience.
Mice	Good luck.
Music	News from an absent friend.
Nuts	If you see them, wealth and happiness. If you eat them, a friend is false.
An ostrich	You will travel.
An owl	Sadness is coming.
A purse	If you find it, success will come. If you lose it, you'll lose a friend.
The Queen	If in her presence, great honour lies ahead.
Roses	Wealth, happiness, long life.
Sailing	Good luck.
Spiders	Financial success.
Tears of sorrow	Joy and laughter.
Umbrellas	Bad luck in business.
Vomiting	If poor, you'll gain money. If rich, you'll lose it.
War	Peaceful times ahead.
Yawning	You are boring to your friends.

They Were First...

by Angus Allan

Roald Amundsen (1872–1928)
A fifty-three day march with dog-sledges took this Norwegian explorer from the Bay of Whales in Antarctica, where he'd landed in his ship, The Fram, to the South Pole. The date—December 14, 1911, and Amundsen had beaten his rival, Captain Scott, in the race to get there. First man to reach the bottom of the world, Amundsen was killed in a flying accident while searching for the lost expedition of another explorer, Nobile, to the North Pole.

Neil Armstrong (Born 1930)
'That's one small step for man, one giant leap for mankind'. These were the words spoken by the astronaut who commanded the Apollo Eleven mission and, on July 21, 1969, became the first man to walk upon the surface of the Moon. Neil Alden Armstrong was born in Wapakoneta, Ohio, of Scottish and German ancestry.

Nancy, Viscountess Astor (1879–1964)
An American by birth (she came from Danville, Virginia) Nancy Astor entered British politics and succeeded her husband as Unionist member for the Sutton Division of Plymouth on November 28, 1919. Just three days later she became the first woman to take her seat in the House of Commons. A champion of women's rights, Lady Astor was an active political hostess between the wars, and it is said that much government policy of the nineteen thirties was decided at her Cliveden house parties.

Roger Bannister (Born 1929)
Twenty or so years ago, the most coveted achievement in athletics—the breaking of the four-minute mile barrier—was realised by Doctor Roger Gilbert Bannister. He did it at the Iffley Road track, Oxford,
on May 6, 1954, clocking a time of three minutes fifty-nine point four seconds to become a legend in his own time!

Christiaan Barnard (Born 1922)
On December 3, 1967, the world was staggered to hear that this South African Professor of Surgery had performed the first ever successful transplant of a human heart. It happened at the Groote Schuur Hospital, Cape Town, and the patient Louis Washkansky, survived eighteen days. Another of Barnard's patients, Philip Blaiberg, lived for twenty months after this incredible operation.

Alexander Graham Bell (1847–1922)
Bell was the Scottish-born physicist and inventor, a naturalised American, who in 1876 invented the telephone. The machine—perhaps the greatest ever advance in personal communication—came out of Bell's researches into speech mechanics that he'd carried out while training teachers of the deaf. Today, there are well over two hundred million telephones in the world.

Enrico Caruso (1873–1921)
The greatest name in the annals of Opera, this Italian tenor was the first singer to owe international success to the gramophone. But Caruso, born in Naples, has the distinction, in this disc-
orientated age, of being the first man to record a million seller. His rendering of Vesti la Giubba (On With the Motley) came out in November 1902, and is still on the lists today!

Jacques-Yves Cousteau (Born 1910)
The man whose name is almost synonymous with underwater exploration began diving with goggles while in the French Navy, in 1936. At Sanary-sur-Mer, in the summer of 1943, Cousteau put on a compressed air aqualung apparatus of his own design and, as colleagues watched, plunged into the sea to make the first ever aqualung dive. His researches have since opened up a whole new world to mankind.

Marie Curie (1867–1934)
This Polish-born French chemist pioneered, with her husband Pierre, the earliest researches into radioactivity. It was Marie who discovered that the Uranium ore, pitchblende, contained minute quantities of an element which the Curies eventually isolated and called radium. Marie's own life ended in tragedy, for exposure to radium—so important in the field of medicine—gave her leukaemia.

Thomas Alva Edison (1847–1931)
An American inventor with more than a thousand patents to his credit, Edison is best remembered for his phonograph, which he constructed in 1877. This one-time newsboy was the first to record and play back
sound, using a foil cylinder. And the first words ever to be recorded by man? 'Mary had a little lamb'!

Arthur Fitzgibbon (1845–   ?)
Not the first to win a Victoria Cross—Britain's highest award for gallantry, instituted in 1856, but certainly the first and youngest *boy* ever to win one was Hospital Apprentice Arthur Fitzgibbon. At the age of fifteen, he gained his V.C. at the Taku Forts, North China, in 1860, while serving with the 67th (Hampshire) Regiment. He must have been something of an individualist, later being dismissed (as an Assistant Surgeon) for insubordination!

Yuri Gagarin (1934–1968)
Russian air-force pilot and cosmonaut, Yuri Alekseyevich Gagarin became the first man in space when his space vehicle *Vostok 1* completed a single orbit of Earth on April 12, 1961. At a maximum speed of 17,560 mph and a maximum altitude of 203.2 miles, Major Gagarin earned a place in history, awards of Hero of the Soviet Union and the Order of Lenin, and the admiration of people the world over. Tragically, he was killed in a plane crash near Moscow on March 27, 1968.

Johannes Gutenberg (1398–1468)
A German goldsmith, Gutenberg is credited with being the first man to print with movable type. A development of woodblock techniques used in making playing cards and prints, his invention was more or less paralleled in other parts of Europe during the mid-fourteenth century, but Gutenberg and his partner, Johann Fust, were certainly the first to set up a large-scale printing house, at Mainz. His bible, produced about 1455, is the earliest and most famous volume ever printed by mechanical means.

Auguste Lumière (1862–1954)
A pioneer of the cinema as entertainment, Lumière (with the assistance of his brother Louis) constructed a camera and projector and became the first to make and show films to the public. It was in the Scribe Hotel, Paris, on December 28, 1895, that interested people paid one franc each to come and see ten short movies—including such items as 'Baby's Breakfast', and 'Arrival of a Train'.

Nicéphore Niepce (1765–1833)
A retired French army officer, this man with the unlikely name began experimenting with light-sensitive chemicals and, after a good deal of trial and error, took the first successful photograph in 1826—a view from his workshop at Chalon-sur-Saône. His 'film' was a pewter plate covered with bitumen dissolved in oil of lavender—a mixture which hardened on exposure to light. Unaffected surfaces were simply washed clean after the exposure—which took eight hours! Niepce's researches were continued after his death by his partner, Louis Daguerre.

Robert Peary (1856–1920)
This American explorer is generally credited with being the first man to reach the North Pole. An attempt in 1905 ended in failure, but in 1909, Peary finally succeeded in reaching the Pole, together with a negro servant and four Eskimos.

Wilhelm Röntgen (1845–1923)
Winner of the first Nobel Prize for Physics, Wilhelm Conrad Röntgen had discovered, in 1895, X-rays. Of prime importance in medicine, both for diagnostic photography and for radiation treatment, in engineering for stress tests in metals, and in general science for analysis, X-rays are electro-magnetic radiations, which Röntgen produced in gas-discharge tubes.

Joshua Slocum (1844–1909)
The first man to complete a solo circumnavigation of the World, Captain Joshua Slocum, left Newport, Rhode Island, in his 10 metre sloop *Spray,* and returned three years, two months and two days later, having made a voyage of 46,000 miles. It was a journey of incredible danger—more especially so since Slocum was a non-swimmer. Unfortunately, he attempted to repeat his achievement in 1909—and set sail, never to be seen again.

Norkay Tenzing (Born 1914)
Towering above his home in the Himalayan State of Nepal, Everest, the world's highest mountain, had always fascinated Norkay Tenzing. And on May 29, 1953, as a Sherpa, or guide, to Sir John Hunt's expedition, he became the first man, alongside Sir Edmund Percival Hillary, to set foot on its summit. The ascent, to the height of 8,847 m won Sherpa Tenzing the George Medal and a place in history.

Valentina Tereshkova (Born 1937)
The first woman to venture into space, Tereshkova was launched in the Soviet spacecraft *Vostok 6* from Baikonur, to complete over forty-eight orbits before she was brought down again after her flight of almost three days. There can be no greater proof of the fact that woman is man's equal, but Valentina was quick to prove that she was no tough-nut amazon. In October of the same year, she married fellow Cosmonaut Andreyan Nikolayev. They did *not* honeymoon in space.

Richard Trevithick (1771–1833)
In 1804—ten years before George Stephenson's successful experiments—the English engineer Trevithick constructed a locomotive at the Pen-y-darren ironworks, near Merthyr Tydfil and ran it, with five wagons, ten tons of iron and seventy passengers, over nine miles of track. It was the first steam railway, and although the track was unequal to the strain, Trevithick had successfully proved the all-important principle that contact between steel wheels and steel rails would permit traction.

Matthew Webb (1848–1883)
Born near Dawley, in Shropshire, this Captain of Merchant Marine learned to swim when he was seven. It was in 1875 that he announced to an incredulous England that he intended to swim the Channel—'without any artificial aid'. His first attempt, on August 12, failed—but undaunted, he took to the water again twelve days later.

After an astonishing battle lasting twenty-one and three-quarter hours, he landed two hundred metres west of Calais harbour, utterly exhausted, but triumphant. He had carried out what The Times called 'a very amazing and entirely unprecedented feat'!

Orville Wright (1871–1948)
The first controlled, continuous power-driven flight took place at Kitty Hawk, North Carolina, on December 17, 1903, when Orville Wright—ex-bicycle manufacturer—flew his chain-driven aircraft Flyer 1 at a speed of eight mph and a height of up to 3·6 m for twelve seconds. He was watched by his partner and brother, Wilbur, and a squad of U.S. Coastguards. Twelve seconds doesn't sound much—but the Wright brothers went on to become the most famous of aviation's pioneers. Together, they won the Michelin Trophy of 1908 with a flight of seventy-seven miles in two hours and twenty minutes.

MIGHTY MAGPIE GINGER BEER

INGREDIENTS

The Yeast Mixture:
55g (2oz) fresh baker's yeast
2 level tablespoons ground ginger
2 level tablespoons caster sugar
¼lit (½ pint) water

To Add to the Yeast Mixture:
10 level teaspoons ground ginger
10 level teaspoons caster sugar

To make the beer:
500g (1lb 2oz) caster sugar
¾lit (1½pt) water
Juice from two lemons
3lit (6pt) water
6 screw-topped bottles (you must use strong glass bottles such as cider bottles or lemonade bottles; do *not* use plastic bottles). A piece of fine muslin (about 20cm (6in) square).

To make the yeast mixture, blend 55g (2oz) yeast and 2 level tablespoons sugar together to make a smooth paste. Add 2 level tablespoons of ground ginger and ¼lit (½pt) water and mix well. Put this mixture in a jar and cover with a napkin.

Every day for ten days add a teaspoon of ground ginger and a teaspoon of caster sugar and stir the mixture.

After ten days you are ready to make the ginger beer. Mix the 500g (1lb 2oz) sugar with the ¾lit (1½pt) of water in a saucepan and bring to the boil stirring constantly. Take the pan off the heat,

add the lemon juice and allow to cool. Pour the ginger mixture in the jar through the fine muslin into the lemon and sugar mixture. Add 3lit (6pt) water, stir constantly and pour the ginger beer into the screw-topped bottles and seal them immediately. It is *vital* you use screw-topped bottles.

You can make more ginger beer by halving the sediment left on the muslin and placing it in two separate jars. Add two level teaspoons of ground ginger and two level teaspoons of caster sugar to each jar and stir well. Continue as before and you can make a new batch of beer every ten days.

— HI THERE!

16

NAME: Mick Robertson

AGE: 29

ZODIAC SIGN: Aquarius

PETS: Piper, a Labrador

CAR: Ford Fairmont

FAVOURITE MUSIC: Electric

FAVOURITE FOOD: Milk Shakes

HOBBIES: Driving Cars

The Magpie File

The Land Ran Red
The Story of the Russian Revolution

BY ANGUS ALLAN

WHILE THE GROWTH OF INDUSTRY PULLED EUROPE INTO THE TWENTIETH CENTURY, THE VASTNESS OF RUSSIA REMAINED OVERWHELMINGLY FEUDAL — MILLIONS OF PEOPLE UNDER THE SOLE CONTROL OF TSAR NICHOLAS II, A MAN PLAGUED BY THE GHASTLY DEFEATS OF THE WAR WITH JAPAN. THE DATE WAS 1905...

SIRE! I BRING A PETITION FROM THE PEASANTS! THEY DEMAND — THAT IS, THEY REQUEST — SOME KIND OF SAY IN OUR COUNTRY'S GOVERNMENT!

I SHALL UPHOLD THE PRINCIPLE OF AUTOCRACY AS DID MY LATE FATHER!

THEY STRESS THEIR **LOYALTY**, SIRE!

I'M GLAD TO HEAR OF IT. THEN LET THEM THINK OF THE WAR!

APPALLED AT THE DEFEAT, DEMORALISED BY THEIR MISERABLE WAGES AND CONDITIONS, WORKERS IN SAINT PETERSBURG STRUCK — AND DEMONSTRATED...

THEN CAME THE DESTRUCTION OF THE RUSSIAN FLEET AT PORT ARTHUR...

WE WANT PEACE!

WE WANT PEACE NOT WAR

DOWN WITH AUTOCRACY

DOWN WITH WAR

PEACE

THE TSAR MUST LEARN OF OUR PLIGHT!

FATHER GEORGI GAPON SHALL LEAD US!

SUNDAY, JANUARY 22nd. THEY CALLED IT BLOODY SUNDAY...

DRIVE THEM BACK, THE UNPATRIOTIC CURS! CUT THEM DOWN!

THE MURDEROUS ACTION OF THE TSAR'S GUARDS ONLY FANNED THE FLAMES OF UNREST. IN THE COUNTRY, PEASANTS ROSE UP TO BURN CROPS AND SACK THEIR MASTERS' HOUSES...

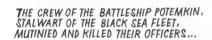

THE CREW OF THE BATTLESHIP POTEMKIN, STALWART OF THE BLACK SEA FLEET, MUTINIED AND KILLED THEIR OFFICERS...

BUT THE REVOLT FIZZLED OUT THROUGH LACK OF CO-ORDINATION. IT DID, HOWEVER, MOVE THE TSAR SUFFICIENTLY TO ACT...

HE'S AGREED TO FORM A DUMA— A GOVERNMENT INCLUDING REPRESENTATIVES ELECTED BY THE PEOPLE!

BUT THE MEANS OF ELECTION! USELESS! THE RICH WILL STILL GOVERN. AND DO WHAT THE TSAR TELLS THEM!

VLADIMIR ILYICH ULYANOV— LATER TO ADOPT THE SURNAME LENIN...

CLEARLY, WE REVOLUTIONARIES CAN DO LITTLE HERE. THE SECRET POLICE WILL BE OUT IN FORCE. I PROPOSE THAT WE LEAVE RUSSIA —UNTIL THE TIME IS RIPE!

I, LEON TROTSKY, AGREE TO THAT MOTION, COMRADE...

SO BEGAN A DECADE OF RELATIVE QUIET. PEASANTRY WAS SUPPRESSED BY SAVAGE TREATMENT...

TO THINK THEY ABOLISHED SERFDOM IN 1861!

I HAVEN'T NOTICED!

INDUSTRIAL WORKERS SLAVED FOR A HANDFUL OF KOPECKS A WEEK...

OUR SO-CALLED REPRESENTATIVES IN THE DUMA GROW FAT, AND SMOKE CIGARS! WHAT DO THEY KNOW OF THIS?

NOTHING! THE VERY KNOWLEDGE WOULD KILL THEM!

IT TOOK THE OUTBREAK OF WORLD WAR I TO FETCH THE LAST STRAW FOR THE CAMEL'S BACK. CONSCRIPTION HURLED PEASANTS TO THE FRONT... AND TO DEATH...

WE ARE LOST! LOST!

BAD TRAINING WORSE RIFLES! NO BULLETS! OUR LEADERS EXPECT US TO WORK THEIR MIRACLES!

DISCONTENT WAS RIFE. AND ON FEBRUARY 23rd 1917, A SOCIALIST HOLIDAY HONOURING INTERNATIONAL WOMAN'S DAY...

SIRE! THERE HAS BEEN A STRIKE! WORKERS ARE PARADING IN THE STREETS!

ANOTHER 1905..? WHAT DO THEY WANT THIS TIME, MARKOWITZ..?

BREAD!

PEACE!

THE RIGHT TO LIVE AS HUMAN BEINGS!

THE SOLDIERS OF THE SAINT PETERSBURG GARRISON WERE UNCERTAIN. THEY, TOO HAD SIMILAR GRIEVANCES...

BROTHER! WE ONLY WANT OUR RIGHTS! WILL YOU STAND AGAINST US..?

NOT I! I'M SICK OF BEING A PUPPET OF A MINDLESS REGIME! COME, LADS! JOIN OUR COMRADES!

THE TSARIST POLICE WERE SENT IN. RENOWNED FOR THEIR BRUTALITY...

LOOK! THE SOLDIERS ARE ON OUR SIDE! WE'LL CARRY THE DAY YET!

IT SPREAD. HOW IT SPREAD! SEASONED REGIMENTS — THE PAVLOVSKY, THE PREOBRAZHENSKY, THE LITHUANIAN AND THE VOLHYNIAN — BROKE OUT...

IN TWO DAYS, THE MOBS HAD LIBERATED POLITICAL PRISONERS FROM THE CITY JAILS!

THEY TOOK THE TAURIDE PALACE... ESTABLISHED A HEADQUARTERS...

WHO ARE THESE OFFICERS?

PUT THEM TO DEATH!

NO, NO! OUR SYMPATHIES ARE WITH YOU! TAKE US IN—WE'LL ORGANISE EVERYTHING! AN ARSENAL... COMMUNICATIONS... WE'LL GET THIS PLACE ON A WAR FOOTING!

IT'S WHAT WE NEED! LEADERSHIP! AND THESE PEOPLE KNOW HOW!

YOU'RE RIGHT! WE'LL LET THEM LIVE!

FROM THE STRENGTH OF THE TAURIDE THEY FORMED AN ALLIANCE — A 'SOVIET'. THE SOVIET OF WORKERS' AND SOLDIERS' DEPUTIES...

THE NEWS FROM RUSSIA IS GOOD. IT IS TIME YOU WENT BACK THERE, VLADIMIR ILYICH...

RUSSIAN TSAR ABDICATES! BELIEVED MURDERED WITH WHOLE FAMILY BY REVOLUTIONARIES! READ ALL ABOUT IT!

RUSSIAN TSAR Abdicates

THE BEGINNING! A NEW AGE FOR MY COUNTRY... FOR THE WORLD! MAY I HAVE THE STRENGTH TO SURVIVE THE TURMOIL YET TO COME!

TURMOIL! RUSSIA HAD SEEN NOTHING LIKE IT. A PROVISIONAL GOVERNMENT HAD BEEN SET UP—HAND IN HAND WITH THE SOVIET...

THE GOVERNMENT IS A PUPPET—THE SOVIET HAS THE REAL POWER!

BUT THE SOVIET ITSELF IS DIVIDED! BOLSHEVIKS—MENSHEVIKS—SOCIAL REVOLUTIONISTS! WHO WILL TAKE CONTROL?

ONE FACTION WARRED AGAINST ANOTHER. ALEXANDER FYODOROVICH KERENSKY AROSE AS A FIGUREHEAD IN A COALITION GOVERNMENT...

THE WAR AGAINST GERMANY MUST COME FIRST! OUR HONOUR AS RUSSIAN PATRIOTS MUST BE ESTABLISHED! I CALL ON YOU ALL TO SUPPORT ME!

THIS MAN FORGETS THE WISHES OF THE PEOPLE, LENIN... WE COULD DEPOSE HIM...

NOT YET, LEON. WE BOLSHEVIKS ARE IN A MINORITY... WE MUST STILL BIDE OUR TIME...

KERENSKY FEARED LENIN, TROTSKY AND THEIR ASSOCIATES. SO DID GENERAL KORNILOV, COMMANDER OF THE SAINT PETERSBURG FORCES AND THE DARLING OF THE RIGHT-WING MEMBERS OF THE COALITION...

YOU CONTROL THE SAVAGE DIVISION, GENERAL! THOSE WILD CAUCASIAN MOUNTAINEERS WOULD TAKE SAINT PETERSBURG FOR YOU... KILL KERENSKY. AND DO AWAY WITH THE BOLSHEVIKS!

AND PLACE ME IN POWER. IT'S A TEMPTING THOUGHT!

A THOUGHT THAT LED HIM TO DEATH. HIS 'SAVAGE DIVERSION' ATTACKED... AND WAS WON OVER BY THE CITIZENRY!

JOIN US! LET YOUR WAR-CRY BE OURS!

BREAD!

PEACE! LAND!

AS FOR LENIN, HE HAD ONCE MORE BEEN FORCED TO FLEE. HE WAS IN FINLAND.

THAT KERENSKY! SO I RETURNED TO RUSSIA FROM GERMANY, IN EXCHANGE FOR POLITICAL PRISONERS. AND HE SMEARED MY NAME—TELLING PEOPLE I WAS A SPY FOR THE KAISER!

KERENSKY'S DAYS ARE NUMBERED! OUR BOLSHEVIKS HAVE CONTROL OF THE SOVIETS IN SAINT PETERSBURG AND MOSCOW!

GOOD NEWS AT LAST. SHALL WE GO, MY FRIEND? PERHAPS THIS TIME I WILL RETURN TO STAY...

IT WAS OCTOBER 21st, 1917. AND THE END CAME ALMOST ABSURDLY SIMPLY. AT A STROKE, THE BOLSHEVIK SOVIET OF SAINT PETERSBURG DECLARED THE GOVERNMENT DISSOLVED.

COMRADE TROTSKY— WE HAVE ONLY TO TAKE THE ARSENAL OF PETER-PAUL, AND ENTIRE VICTORY IS OURS!

UM. AN ARSENAL WHOSE TROOPS ARE LOYAL TO OUR LATE AND UNLAMENTED GOVERNMENT. LET US NOT BOTHER TO WASTE BULLETS!

A GREAT ORATOR, LEON DAVIDOVITCH TROTSKY CONQUERED THE BASTION BY SHEER ELOQUENCE. HIS 20,000 RED GUARDS—ARMED WORKERS DIDN'T EVEN NEED TO COCK THEIR GUNS...

A GREAT ACHIEVEMENT. BUT YOU'VE HEARD THAT KERENSKY HAS MASSED TROOPS TO ATTEMPT A COUNTER REVOLUTION YET AGAIN!

LET HIM. NOTHING WILL STOP US NOW, COMRADE. NOTHING!

TROTSKY WAS RIGHT. LENIN CONDUCTED AN ARMISTICE WITH GERMANY, AND THE PEACE STRENGTHENED THE BOLSHEVIK CAUSE IN RUSSIA. KERENSKY'S FORCES WERE DEFEATED ON OCTOBER 30th...

AND THE LONG, COMPLEX TURMOIL OF THE RUSSIAN REVOLUTION WAS OVER! THE STAGE WAS SET FOR THE EMERGENCE OF THE U.S.S.R. FROM FEUDALISM INTO THE FRONT RANKS OF WORLD POWER!

Printing on paper

HAVE YOU EVER THOUGHT OF HAVING
PERSONALISED WRITING PAPER? HERE ARE
TWO METHODS OF MAKING SOME — BOTH
ARE MESSY SO COVER ALL WORKING
SURFACES WITH NEWSPAPER BEFORE YOU
START!

POTATO PRINTS

USING A TABLE KNIFE, CUT A POTATO
IN HALF. NOW CHIP AWAY AT THE CUT
SURFACE OF THE POTATO TO LEAVE
A RAISED DESIGN (SEE DIAGRAM). DIP THE DESIGN IN
POSTER OR POWDER PAINT AND PRESS IT ON TO A
PIECE OF PAPER.

STENCILS

DRAW A DESIGN ON TO A PIECE OF CARD
AND CUT IT OUT WITH SCISSORS. PUT THE CARD
OVER A PIECE OF PAPER AND HOLDING IT WITH
ONE HAND, PAINT OVER THE HOLE WITH
THE OTHER. TO DO THIS YOU CAN USE
A PAINT BRUSH, A SPONGE DIPPED IN
PAINT OR A SPRAY CAN.

Printing on fabric

USING THESE TWO METHODS OF PRINTING YOU CAN BRIGHTEN UP OLD CLOTHES. INSTEAD OF PAINT, USE WATER-BASED FABRIC DYE, FOLLOWING THE MANUFACTURER'S INSTRUCTIONS. REMEMBER TO STUFF THE GARMENT WITH NEWSPAPER BEFORE YOU START, OTHERWISE THE DYE WILL SOAK THROUGH ON TO THE BACK OF THE CLOTHING. ASK YOUR PARENTS FOR PERMISSION BEFORE STARTING — ESPECIALLY IF YOU ARE PRINTING ON CLOTHES!

HAVE FUN!

HOW A BOOK IS PRINTED...

1
WHEN THE AUTHOR HAS WRITTEN THE BOOK, HE TYPES IT OUT AND SENDS IT TO THE PUBLISHER. THE PUBLISHER READS IT AND DECIDES WHETHER OR NOT TO PUBLISH IT.

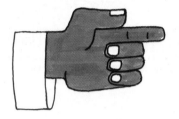

THE MIGHTY MAGPIE
The zoological nam
is Pica pica, and
noted for its nois
pilfering habits.
name for Magpie is
a mixture of ' Mar
meaning Black and

MANUSCRIPT

2 DESIGN
THE DESIGNER DECIDES THE PROPORTIONS OF THE BOOK: THAT IS THE SIZE AND SHAPE, AND WHERE THE PICTURES SHOULD BE AND THE SIZE OF TYPE. AT THIS POINT, THE PUBLISHER, PRINTER AND DESIGNER DECIDE HOW THE BOOK SHOULD BE PRINTED

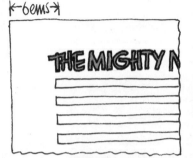

8 CORRECTIONS
THE PAGES OF THE BOOK ARE THEN MADE UP WITH THE METAL TYPE AND BLOCKS IN POSITION. A ROUGH PRINT IS MADE, ALL THE PEOPLE CONCERNED WITH MAKING THE BOOK THEN MAKE SURE THAT THERE ARE NO MISTAKES IN THE PRINT. IF THERE ARE, THE PRINTER PUTS THEM RIGHT.

9/h As they go out to might be thinkin or watching the wives and childr complete strange full time job as volunteers. The oars and sails

9
WHEN EVERYBODY IS SATISFIED THAT THE BOOK IS READY TO BE PRINTED, THE PAGES ARE ARRANGED INTO A PATTERN ON THE PRINTING MACHINE, SO THAT WHEN THEY ARE PRINTED, THE PAPER WILL FOLD WITH THE PAGES IN THE RIGHT ORDER.

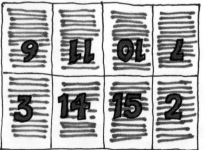

IMPOSITION

7 COLOUR
THE COLOUR PHOTOGRAPHS AND ILLUSTRATIONS HAVE TO BE TREATED IN MUCH THE SAME WAY AS THE ONES JUST DESCRIBED, INASMUCH AS THEY HAVE TO BE BROKEN UP INTO TINY DOTS. BUT IN ADDITION THEY HAVE TO BE BROKEN DOWN INTO FOUR BASIC COLOURS. THIS IS DONE WITH FILTERS PHOTOGRAPHICALLY. THE BASIC COLOURS ARE YELLOW, RED, BLUE AND BLACK. COPPER PLATES ARE MADE, AND WHEN THE FOUR SETS OF DIFFERENT DOTS ARE PRINTED OVER EACH OTHER, THEY RE-FORM THE PICTURE.

10 PRINTING
THE TYPE AND BLOCKS ARE INKED WITH A ROLLER, THE PAPER WRAPS AROUND A CYLINDER WHICH MOVES ACROSS THE TYPE, PRESSING HARD. THE INK IS TRANSFERRED FROM THE TYPE TO THE PAPER — YOU NOW HAVE PRINTED PAGES!

CYLINDER
INK
PAPER

3 WE WILL SHOW THE LETTERPRESS METHOD OF PRINTING WHICH IS A 'RELIEF' METHOD OF PRINTING LIKE POTATO CUTS AND LINO-CUTS PRINTING, WHICH YOU MAY HAVE DONE.

4 THE DESIGNER SENDS THE MANUSCRIPT TO THE PRINTER WITH DRAWINGS (CALLED LAYOUTS) AND INSTRUCTIONS HOW THE METAL TYPE SHOULD BE 'SET' OR POSITIONED. THE TYPE HAS TO BE MADE INTO LINES THE WRONG WAY ROUND SO THAT THE PRINT FROM IT SHALL BE THE RIGHT WAY.

TYPE

6 BLOCKS IF THE PHOTOGRAPHS OR DRAWINGS IN A TONE ARE TO BE PRINTED, THE WHOLE SURFACE OF THE SUBJECT MUST BE BROKEN UP INTO DOTS OF VARYING SIZES. (LOOK AT THE PHOTOGRAPHS IN THIS BOOK WITH A MAGNIFYING GLASS – YOU WILL SEE THAT THEY ARE MADE UP OF THOUSANDS OF TINY DOTS.) THE DOTTED PICTURES ARE TRANSFERRED TO COPPER, INTO WHICH THE SPACES BETWEEN THE DOTS ARE ETCHED

5 THE DESIGNER ALSO DECIDES HOW AND WHERE THE BOOK SHOULD HAVE PICTURES AND ASKS AN ILLUSTRATOR TO DO THE DRAWINGS AND A PHOTOGRAPHER TO TAKE PHOTOGRAPHS

ILLUSTRATION

11 BINDING WHEN THE INK IS DRY, THE PAPER IS FOLDED – THE PAGES ARE ALL IN ORDER. THEY ARE THEN SEWN ALONG THE FOLD. THE EDGES ARE TRIMMED WITH A CUTTING MACHINE, AND THE PAGES, IN 16 PAGE BUNDLES ARE GLUED INTO A CARDBOARD COVER.

12 THE FINISHED BOOKS ARE TAKEN TO THE PUBLISHER WHO ORGANIZES THEIR DISTRIBUTION TO BOOKSHOPS ALL OVER THE COUNTRY.

DISTRIBUTION

PEDALPOWER

by Sue Fox

Many of you reading this book will be able to ride a bicycle. But can you ride it properly? Equally important, do you know how to look after your bike without having to ask your parents or the man at the cycle shop for help? Here is a very basic guide to some of the things you will need to know.

Buying a bike

This doesn't necessarily have to be a new one as they can cost a great deal of money. Yours may well be the most expensive present you will ever have. Look after it and it will give you years of pleasure. You might grow out of your bike one day, but, if you have cared for it, the bike won't have worn out.

Good second hand bikes are not difficult to find. Check your nearest cycle shop first. They may well have something in stock. Look at the 'For Sale' Advertisements in the local paper. Ask friends whose brothers and sisters are a few years older than you. Their bikes may be too small for them and just right for you.

It is essential that your bike is the right size.

A cyclist has to be able to control the bike in any circumstances. This is impossible, and dangerous, if you are uncomfortable. If the frame is too small, you will be cramped when pedalling and unable to manoeuvre the bike correctly. If only the tip of a toe reaches the ground, then the saddle is too high. Ideally, you should be able to sit on the saddle and touch the ground with the ball of your foot. Saddles and handlebars are adjustable. It is well worth spending time trying various heights until you find the one which suits you best. Be comfortable. Be safe.

Is it roadworthy?

You have your bicycle. Before riding it, make sure that it is completely roadworthy. Regardless of whether it is brand new or second hand, check the brakes, chain, tyres, lights. A bell is a good idea too! All moving parts must be properly adjusted regularly and well oiled. Be careful with the oil can. Use just a little and be sure not to let it run on to the tyres or rims. If this happens and you don't wipe off the oil, you might easily have a nasty skid, or your brakes will let you down. Check your bike often. Be methodical about it. Keep your Mighty Magpie Book and this Bike Guide handy, it will

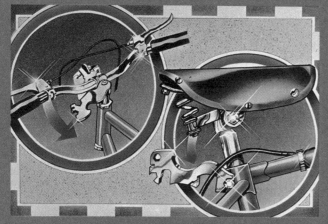

Above: **The saddle** *Using an all-purpose spanner loosen the nut on the seat post clamp to adjust the height of the saddle, to adjust its position loosen the nut underneath the peak of the saddle. Don't forget to tighten the nuts again afterwards!* **The handlebars** *To adjust the height of the handlebars loosen the locking ring on the head tube. Don't forget to tighten the nuts again afterwards!*

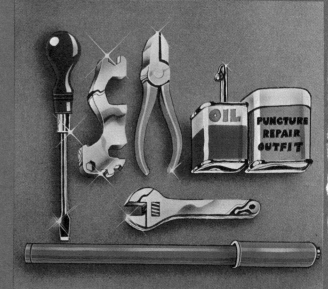

Above: A shining new bike, only careful maintenance will ensure it stays in this condition.

Left: A selection of useful tools. Left to right, a screwdriver, an all-purpose spanner, pliers, oil, a puncture repair kit. Below, an adjustable spanner and a pump.

help you stick to a good routine.

Basic tools

There are a few basic tools you should collect which should help with bicycle maintenance. Most of them are probably at home already. Keep the ones you will need regularly in a specially marked tin or box. Once you are used to doing minor jobs at home, you will save time and money. But if there is something you aren't sure about ask. If your parents aren't sure either, then please go to the cycle shop for expert advice. Don't ever leave this to the last minute. You don't want to have to drop out of a special ride with friends because your bike isn't 100 per cent safe to use. When doing repairs yourself, if you take things off the bike, put them on paper or cloth in the order in which you removed them. It will make it easier to put them back in the correct order.

Clothes and accessories

It is important to be as uncluttered as possible. Never wear long scarves when cycling. These can be lethal and get stuck in the pedals or wheels. Capes are very good in bad weather, but you must be careful not to wear one which is massive and will flap about and possibly get caught up in the wheels. Trousers are the best cycling gear—girls please don't wear long skirts. Make sure your shoe laces (if you have them) are neatly tied or they will get tangled in the pedals. Warm socks and gloves and plenty of layers help to keep you warm in cold weather.

Always use a proper bicycle bag which can be attached securely to the bike. Here you can keep drinks and sandwiches for long journeys. Don't ever strap any old bag around the handlebars—this is very dangerous, and never carry anything heavy or awkward on your back.

Don't forget that you need to be seen at night time. In winter this will mean the time you come out of school. Make sure your lights are really bright, and wear something white, or reflective patches on your clothes. In the daytime drivers can see you better if you wear something fluorescent

Road safety

Just because you are able to balance successfully on two wheels doesn't mean that you can actually ride a bike. It requires experience and skill to ride well. To be really safe, and to get the most fun out of using your tip-top cycle, you need to be aware of three basic things:

1 The Law In the eyes of the Law, a cycle is a carriage, which is an old-fashioned word for a vehicle. A local Government Act of 1888 gave cyclists the right to use the highways along with other vehicles. Today, of course, roads and traffic are much busier than they were 90 years ago, so it is even more important to obey the laws which apply to every kind of vehicle. Behave responsibly. Never do anything that you wouldn't expect other drivers or cyclists to do. Never go so fast that you are a danger both to yourself and other people. Always obey the signals given by policemen, traffic wardens and traffic lights. Be alert to all road signs. Never, never cycle on the footpath.

It is essential that you and your bike can always be seen by other road users. If you are out in the dark, the bike must show a bright white light to the front, and have both a red light and a red reflector on the rear. These have to be fixed on to the bicycle itself. Never clip a light to your clothing or your bicycle bag.

2 'Language of the Road' Before using the roads, you must know how to read road signs, road markings and the signals to give to or receive from other cyclists and motorists. Road markings are often a warning of possible hazards ahead. Signs indicate the sort of road or traffic to expect. Clear and correct signals enable road users to tell one another what they intend to do, making the road safer for everyone.

3 The Highway Code Much of the training for the National Cycling Proficiency Certificate is based on this. A copy of the Highway Code costs only 12p from most bookshops and you are given one free when you start your training. It will answer virtually any question you may have about road usage. Admittedly, there is a

a *Below: Arm signals. Left to right: I intend to move out or turn right, I intend to move in to the left or turn left, I intend to slow down or stop.*

b *Below: Some useful road signs Clockwise starting at the top: No entry; T junction; Stop and give way; Level crossing without gate or barrier ahead; No cycling or moped-riding; Steep hill upwards; No right turn; Cross roads; No pedestrians; Traffic merges from the left.*

a

b

lot to learn, but you will never be a good cyclist—or, for that matter, a motorist—if you are not prepared to study it. How many of the above signs do you recognise?

If you are over nine years old, you can train for the official National Cycling Proficiency Test which will give you a sound basic training in safe cycling. The Test is sponsored by the Royal Society for the Prevention of Accidents (ROSPA for short). It is a national scheme which operates throughout the country. Specially-trained road safety officers, police and teachers run the instruction courses which are held in safe, open spaces of school playgrounds or under close supervision on quiet roads.

Many head teachers, before they give permission for you to use your bicycle for travelling to and from school, expect you to have passed the National Test. Younger children can often take part in the training sessions, but to qualify for the test itself you must have had your ninth birthday. You can find out how you can take the National Cycling Proficiency Test from your local Road Safety Officer, the police or your school. It's a tough test, which covers bicycle maintenance and all aspects of road safety which will help to keep you and your bike in one piece.

It's better to be safe than sorry

Each year there are more than two thousand really serious accidents involving child cyclists,

and many less severe accidents as well, so it is in everybody's interest that you should know as much as possible about how to ride and look after your bike from the word go. The standard of the Test has to be extremely high— considering today's traffic. To gain the Certificate and Badge, you need a minimum of 75 per cent marks in each of five separate sections covered by the Test.

Start off your cycling days knowing how to ride safely on a properly maintained bike, and you may help to reduce the number of accidents. Meanwhile. all you competent bikers could do a great deal to help younger brothers, sisters and their friends to learn some good bicycle sense. If you want more information write to the *National Cycling Officer, ROSPA, Cannon House, The Priory Queensway, Birmingham B 4 6BS Tel: 021 233-2461* or contact your local road safety officer. (Diagram courtesy of ROSPA.)

Keep your bicycle in good order

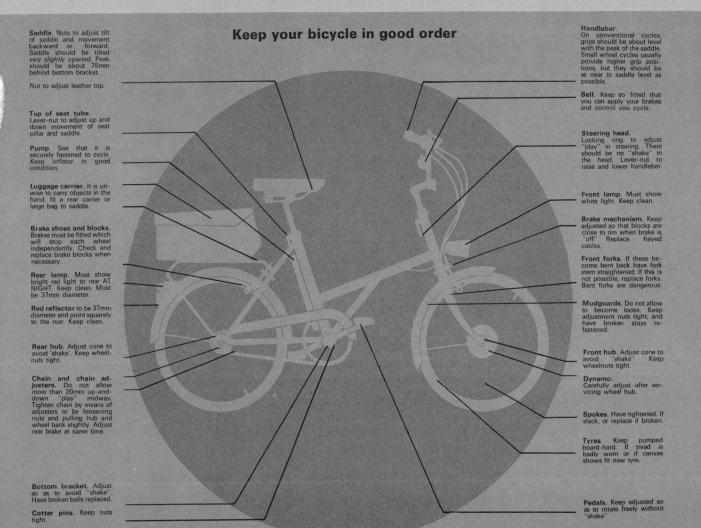

Saddle. Nuts to adjust tilt of saddle and movement backward or forward. Saddle should be tilted *very slightly* upward. Peak should be about 75mm behind bottom bracket.

Nut to adjust leather top.

Top of seat tube. Lever-nut to adjust up and down movement of seat pillar and saddle.

Pump. See that it is securely fastened to cycle. Keep inflator in good condition.

Luggage carrier. It is unwise to carry objects in the hand, fit a rear carrier or large bag to saddle.

Brake shoes and blocks. Brakes must be fitted which will stop each wheel independently. Check and replace brake blocks when necessary.

Rear lamp. Must show bright red light to rear AT NIGHT. Keep clean. Must be 37mm diameter.

Red reflector to be 37mm diameter and point squarely to the rear. Keep clean.

Rear hub. Adjust cone to avoid 'shake'. Keep wheel-nuts tight.

Chain and chain adjusters. Do not allow more than 20mm up-and-down "play" midway. Tighten chain by means of adjusters or by loosening nuts and pulling hub and wheel back slightly. Adjust rear brake at same time.

Bottom bracket. Adjust so as to avoid "shake". Have broken balls replaced.

Cotter pins. Keep nuts tight.

Handlebar. On conventional cycles. grips should be about level with the peak of the saddle. Small wheel cycles usually provide higher grip positions, but they should be as near to saddle level as possible.

Bell. Keep so fitted that you can apply your brakes and control you cycle.

Steering head. Locking ring to adjust "play" in steering. There should be no "shake" in the head. Lever-nut to raise and lower handlebar.

Front lamp. Must show white light. Keep clean.

Brake mechanism. Keep adjusted so that blocks are close to rim when brake is "off". Replace frayed cables.

Front forks. If these become bent back have fork stem straightened; If this is not possible, replace forks. Bent forks are dangerous.

Mudguards. Do not allow to become loose. Keep adjustment nuts tight, and have broken stays refastened.

Front hub. Adjust cone to avoid "shake". Keep wheelnuts tight.

Dynamo. Carefully adjust after servicing wheel hub.

Spokes. Have tightened. If slack, or replace if broken.

Tyres. Keep pumped board-hard. If tread is badly worn or if canvas shows fit new tyre.

Pedals. Keep adjusted so as to rotate freely without "shake".

NAME: Jenny Hanley

AGE: 29

ZODIAC SIGN: Leo

FAMILY: One brother, three half-sisters

PETS: None, except for a local friendly blackbird!

CARS: 1960 Porsche Convertible, BMW 1600

FAVOURITE MUSIC: Loud!

FAVOURITE FOOD: Lots!

HOBBIES: Driving, tapestry, cooking, fishing

FAVOURITE SPORTS PERSONALITY: Barry Sheene

TOP SECRET

The Magpie File

Make & Do Presents

by Danielle Sacher

PAPER BOUQUET

TO MAKE A BUNCH OF 20 FLOWERS YOU WILL NEED:
20 PIECES OF CRÊPE PAPER 30 X 7·5 cm (12 in X 3 in)
IN LOTS OF DIFFERENT COLOURS.
A LARGE SHEET OF COLOURED CELLOPHANE PAPER.
SOME FLORIST'S WIRE.
A THIN STICK ABOUT 30 cm (12 in) LONG.
PLIERS.
THREAD.
SCISSORS.

① CUT THE CELLOPHANE INTO 15 cm (6 in) SQUARES

② SCREW THE CELLOPHANE INTO A KNOB AND TIE A PIECE OF THREAD AROUND THE BOTTOM OF IT TO KEEP IT TIGHT.

③ ARRANGE A STRIP OF CRÊPE PAPER LOOSELY AROUND THE CELLOPHANE AND FIX IT IN PLACE WITH WIRE.

④ TIGHTEN THE WIRE WITH A PAIR OF PLIERS AND LEAVE A 'STALK' 15 cm (6 in) LONG.

⑤ OPEN UP THE CRÊPE PAPER TO MAKE A FLOWER SHAPE.

⑥ MAKE ABOUT 20 FLOWERS IN THIS WAY AND THEN WIND EACH WIRE STALK AROUND THE STICK UNTIL YOU HAVE A BUNCH OF PAPER FLOWERS.

POTATO HEDGEHOG.

YOU WILL NEED: 1 LARGE POTATO, A SMALL AMOUNT OF EARTH, 4 USED MATCHSTICKS, 2 DRAWING PINS, 1 LARGE NAIL, A PACKET OF MUSTARD AND CRESS SEED, AN OLD SPOON

① CUT THE POTATO IN HALF AND SCOOP OUT THE CENTRE OF ONE HALF WITH A SPOON.

② PUSH 4 USED MATCHSTICKS INTO THE BOTTOM FOR LEGS, 2 DRAWING PINS AND A NAIL INTO THE FRONT FOR EYES AND A NOSE.

③ PUT SOME EARTH IN THE POTATO, SPRINKLE THE MUSTARD AND CRESS SEEDS ON TOP AND COVER THEM WITH A THIN LAYER OF EARTH.

④ WATER LIGHTLY AND WATCH THE MUSTARD AND CRESS SEEDS GROW UNTIL IT LOOKS JUST LIKE A HEDGEHOG!

33

double exposure

by Geoffrey Morgan

When they reached the top of the dyke wall Jeremy dropped full length into the grass. He pulled down his cousin beside him.

'Don't make a sound, Ann,' he whispered urgently. 'Just the other side, fishing in the mud, is one of the rarest birds in these parts—the avocet. I've never got close enough to photograph one before.' As he spoke he levelled up his camera with the top of the wall and, resting on his elbows, focused it on his target.

Ann edged forward through the long, salt-tanged grass, close to her companion. The Suffolk marshes were a new experience for her, and only in the last few days since she had been staying with Jeremy had she come to know the uncanny thrill of watching and stalking the many varieties of wild seabirds that inhabited the lonely creeks and marshland surrounding her cousin's farmhouse home.

As Jeremy clicked the shutter Ann peered over the wall. She saw the boat first. It was anchored in the narrow, twisting creek a few yards from where the tide lapped the mudflat below the wall. It was a white, heavy-timbered craft with the lines of a fishing boat. Ann noticed that the deck was deserted though the companion-hatch was open.

The strange bird that had so excited Jeremy stood at the water's edge in line with the boat. It was a small creature with a long upward curving beak which it was stabbing into the mud. Ann failed to see why her cousin should attach so much importance to it. She was more interested in the boat, and as her attention returned to it she suddenly wondered why it should be moored in such an isolated place. They were nearly three miles from the village and between them and the sea stretched a vast expanse of marsh and water completely barren of human life and habitation. It was hardly the spot to moor a boat. What had brought the owner there?

'Oh—blow! End of film!' exclaimed Jeremy softly.

Her cousin's sudden announcement broke into Ann's wandering thoughts, and she watched while he reloaded the camera.

'Whose boat is that?' Ann asked quietly.

'Ssh!' was her cousin's response as he concentrated on his subject again. He pressed the shutter release once more and almost simultaneously the bird rose startled into the air and flew off at speed across the creek.

The next moment the cause of the bird's sudden flight hove into view. He was a short thick-set

man with a round, deeply-tanned face. He wore a
blue fisherman's jersey and the legs of his rough
serge trousers were stuffed into the tops of
seaboots. He bobbed up from the creek just at the
point where the dyke wall turned sharply, and
moved towards them as they stood up on the path
topping the wall. He stared at Jeremy's camera,
his mouth breaking into a smile.

'Did ye get it?' he asked, nodding in the
direction the avocet had gone.

'I think so,' Jeremy said guardedly.

'Heard they were nesting again in these parts.
Been here for days waiting to get one on film then,
when it finally appears—what happens?'

The cousins stared at him expectantly.

'Drops me camera in the river! Only this
morning, it was.'

'I'm sorry. That's awful bad luck,' Jeremy said.
'But you'll get another chance.'

'That's the trouble,' he moaned. 'We won't be
here much longer. The chap I've hired the boat to
goes back to London tomorrow. He's one of these
'ere naturalists and writes for the papers. Had to
go into Ledbury today and left me with his camera
and strict instructions to photograph the avocet
when it appeared. It was for a country magazine.
He'll raise the very devil when he knows I've
bungled it.'

'But he won't know the bird has been here,'
suggested Ann.

'That's true,' he agreed. 'But he'll know I've
ruined his camera.' He paused, looking slyly at the
cousins. 'If I could produce a film with the bird
on it I shouldn't be likely to lose one of my best
customers,' he said thoughtfully then suddenly
beamed at Jeremy. 'Tell you what, boy, you
wouldn't be willing to sell me your film, would ye
now? I'd pay a good price.'

Jeremy pretended to show surprise; but he had
already guessed what was in the stranger's mind.
What other reason was there for his lengthy
explanation? His brain grappled rapidly with the
situation. He had one exposed film in his pocket
which contained the first shot of the avocet. The
new film in his camera held the second shot. If he
sold the new film he would still have a photograph
for himself and the money would enable him to
buy new rolls of film. Jeremy's astute young mind
readily appreciated these facts as he smiled up at
the stranger.

'I don't really want to part with it,' he said.
'But what sort of offer had you in mind?'

Riding their cycles along the cart track to the

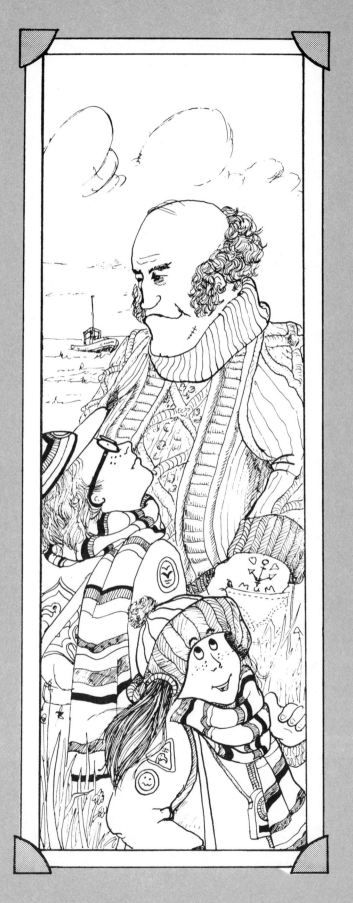

village was no pleasure ride, but Jeremy and Ann were too excited to notice the ruts and potholes over which they bounced.

'Fancy giving you five pounds for one snapshot!' Ann repeated incredulously. 'He must be round the bend.'

'If the film in my pocket doesn't come out I shall go round the bend for parting with it,' Jeremy retorted coolly. 'You don't get a chance to snap an avocet every day.'

'All the same, his story sounds a bit fishy to me. He doesn't look like a man who goes about giving money away. And did you notice . . . there was someone else on the boat? Somebody was peering through the porthole as we left.'

'I didn't see anyone. And, anyway, it's none of our business.' Jeremy dismissed the subject and concentrated on getting to the village as quickly as possible. Just before they reached the main street he pulled in towards the gate of a small cottage set well back from the road.

'What's the idea?' Ann asked, puzzled. 'I thought you were going to get your film developed.'

'So I am. This is where I get it done. Sergeant Lamb lives here.'

'Sergeant Lamb—?'

'Ex-sergeant,' Jeremy interrupted, correcting himself with a grin. 'He's retired from the police and now his main hobby is photography. He always develops my films and he usually let's me see him do it.'

Ex-sergeant Lamb's appearance certainly belied his name. He was tall with broad shoulders, and his dark neat moustache gave his face a fierce expression. But when he greeted Jeremy and was introduced to Ann, his manner was kindly and his grey eyes soft. He had just prepared tea and invited his visitors to join him.

Across the table in the cheerful little room Jeremy related his story about the avocet and the stranger from the boat. The sergeant congratulated him on his business transaction, but he was obviously puzzled by the boatman's readiness to part with so much money before he had even seen if Jeremy's picture would come out. However, he made no comment and as soon as tea was over he took them upstairs to his tiny darkroom.

It was nearly an hour later that all three stood back and admired the enlargement Sergeant Lamb had made of what Jeremy considered to be a prize picture; but it was not the bird to which the sergeant drew their attention, it was the boat. The vessel's sweeping lines formed a distinct background to the small central figure, its

heavy features almost over-shadowing Jeremy's rare subject.

'That boat . . .' muttered the sergeant again. 'It strikes a chord somewhere . . .' He moved across the room and began rummaging in an old desk. Presently, he returned with another photograph and placed it next to Jeremy's.

Ann drew a deep breath. 'Why—it looks the same!'

'Except that this is painted white and the one in your photograph looks black,' Jeremy pointed out to their host.

'That's easily fixed,' the sergeant told him. 'I wonder . . .' he mused. 'That man's story . . .' He stared at Jeremy. 'You know, my boy, I don't think your generous buyer wanted your film because the bird is on it. It's because he was scared his boat is in the picture, too.'

'What d'you mean?' Jeremy asked, astonished. 'Where did *your* picture come from?'

The sergeant's eyes twinkled. 'Scotland Yard.' He sat down. 'About six months ago, just before I retired from the Force, a daring robbery occurred in a large house on the Sussex coast. Jewellery to the value of several thousand pounds was stolen and the thieves got away. It was soon discovered that no cars were used in their getaway and a witness came forward and reported that a fishing boat had been anchored off the spot, and about the time of the robbery this witness had seen two men come from the direction of the house, row out to the boat and sail away. Further inquiries revealed that a yachtsman had passed the vessel in the Channel next day and he had been close enough to read her name. She was called *Windfall*.

'An approach to the yachting press was made and it was learned that the boat had been offered for sale a month before. The previous owner was found and he explained that he had bought the boat as a fishing vessel and had converted her to a yacht. He provided the photograph. He had then sold her to a man named Maitland who we were unable to trace.

'Details and copies of the photo were circulated to all police stations around the coast; but we didn't get very far, for a few days later she was reported to have gone down in a gale off Harwich. A lifebuoy with her name on was picked up together with a waterlogged dinghy she had been towing.'

Jeremy's eyes sparkled. 'And you think the sinking was a fake and the boat in my picture is the *Windfall*?'

'I wouldn't like to swear to it,' returned the sergeant cautiously. 'But after your transaction this afternoon and the definite similarity of the boats in the photos, I think it ought to be investigated. Of course, they would have changed the name when they repainted the boat.'

'But why should they moor up here?' Ann wanted to know.

'I think I can explain that,' Sergeant Lamb returned slowly. 'As I told you, the jewellery was worth a lot of money. It was well known stuff belonging to a Lady Carsdale. The police were hot in pursuit. Under those conditions it would be difficult for crooks to dispose of it. No fence would handle it until the hue and cry had died down. It had got to be parked somewhere meantime—what better place than in a boat?' He paused. 'The creeks and marshes in this area are isolated enough. Few people visit them except wildfowlers in winter and a few bird watchers and yachtsmen in the summer. Once the *Windfall* had lost her identity it must have seemed safe enough to moor up in some lonely creek with the excuse that the occupants were studying natural history. Of course, they'd never expect the boat to be photographed—even by accident,' he ended with a grin.

'What are you going to do?' Jeremy asked.

'Investigate.' Sergeant Lamb considered. 'As I shall be working in an unofficial capacity I shall take along the local constable. And just in case we've stumbled on the right track, I'll ring up my friend at Brinklesea and get a Customs launch up the creek.'

'You must let me have a film, Sarge,' Jeremy cried excitedly. 'I shall probably get some even better pictures.'

Their host's expression took on a stern air. 'You've done pretty well so far and kept out of trouble. I can't have you—'

'But,' protested Jeremy firmly, 'if it hadn't been for us you'd—'

'All right. All right,' Sergeant Lamb held up his hand and smiled his resignation. 'But you promise me to keep right in the background at a safe distance or I'll pack you both off home.'

Just as they had promised, Jeremy and Ann hung back as, an hour later, Sergeant Lamb and the constable went forward to the dyke wall fronting the creek after leaving their cycles on the cart track readily available in case of need. Jeremy spotted a grassy hummock that commanded a view of the creek, and led Ann towards it. They threw

themselves flat in the long, spiky grass, but even from the height of their position they were disappointed to find that part of the boat was hidden from view by the twist in the dyke wall. Nevertheless, remembering the sergeant's instructions to remain out of sight, there was nothing for it but to suffer their disappointment and wait until the action began.

Jeremy held his camera at the ready although he knew the time had passed to get good pictures. Already the light was beginning to fade.

Ann's eyes followed the line of the creek until it disappeared behind a point in the marshland. 'How far down is Brinklesea—?' she began, when voices ahead froze the words on her lips. There was a shout and a splash, but even when they raised themselves they could not see what was happening below the dyke wall. Then the rhythmic hum of a powerful motor shattered the stillness and they saw the yacht glide out into the creek and turn towards the sea.

'Wonder what's happened?' whispered Jeremy fearfully.

'They won't get far,' cried his cousin. 'Look! The Customs launch!' She pointed excitedly to the bend in the creek. A long, slim motorboat came full into view, its sharp bows turning the smooth water into a creamy whirl of foam. It set course for the yacht. The *Windfall* went about and made for the other side of the creek. The launch turned to block its way. Once again the yacht changed course while the launch drew closer.

'The yacht's heading for the dyke wall!' exclaimed Jeremy breathlessly. And within another minute, the Customs launch almost alongside, the yacht stuck fast in the mud. They

saw two men leap over the side and scramble up the wall just as Sergeant Lamb and the constable reached the spot. There was a brief fight and the bigger of the fugitives who had tackled Sergeant Lamb, kicked out and sent the ex-policeman sprawling down the wall. Then he ran for the cart track as the men from the launch appeared.

'Look at that!' gasped Jeremy in dismay. 'He's making for the bikes. He's bound to see them.'

'It's the man who bought your film,' Ann muttered. 'They'll never catch him.'

'Jeremy slid down the hummock and sped across the soft boggy ground towards the track as the man jumped on the sergeant's cycle. Almost without thinking he unslung his camera and threw it with all his force at the fugitive's head. It was a lucky shot. It hit the rider just above the right ear. He wobbled, then lost his balance and plunged down the sharp incline into a ditch of reeds and water.

After the Customs Officers had pulled him out and congratulations had been showered on Jeremy, Sergeant Lamb explained that their other prisoner had confessed to the robbery and had told them where the jewellery was hidden in the yacht. But Jeremy was hardly listening. He was stooping down picking up the remains of his camera.

Sergeant Lamb noticed the expression on his face as he showed him the pieces, and he smiled reassuringly.

'Don't let that worry you, Jeremy,' he said gently. 'You'll have the chance of a dozen cameras before the week is out. I forgot to mention,' he added slyly. 'that a little matter of a reward is attached to this case.'

LET'S MAKE A

by Mick Loftus

Sounds easy enough, but there's more to making a record than meets the ear, as the *Magpie* team discovered when we visited the studios and factories of the world's biggest record company—EMI.

The first thing to understand is the difference between *records* and *recording.* A record is mass-produced in a factory on shiny black discs; a recording is made in a studio on sound-sensitive vinyl tape which can be cut up, rearranged and improved until everyone is satisfied with the result. Only then is the tape sent to a disc-cutter who plays the tape and re-records it on to a black disc resembling a record without any grooves. His machine cuts a continuous groove into the disc, starting at the outer edge and working its way towards the centre. This groove, which is narrower than a human hair and can be as long as half a mile on an LP record, wavers from side to side in response to the sounds coming from the tape. The louder the sounds, the more the groove will waver. The art of the disc-cutter is to produce the best possible sound level without making the groove so wavy that it trips the playing arm of the average record player at home. When he has produced a 'master' disc which meets with the approval of all concerned, the record is considered ready for mass-production.

When the master disc arrives at the factory it is cleaned and rinsed thoroughly, because the slightest speck of dirt left in the grooves will be reproduced in every record made. It is then sprayed with chemical solutions which react to coat it with a fine layer of silver, which conducts electricity well. Next it is placed in a bath of nickel sulphamate solution with an electric current running through it. This causes a layer of nickel to form on top of the silver, a layer which takes about four hours to reach the required thickness of 0·46 of a millimetre. The master is removed, rinsed and dried. Then it is carefully prised away from its nickel shell, which has become an exact replica of the master, but in reverse or 'negative' form.

1 A disc cutting engineer examines a master disc in the cutting room at the EMI studios.

3 The lower stamper in position on the automatic compression moulding press.

RECORD

2 The silver and nickel 'mould' is prised away from the master disc.

4 The vinyl sandwiched between two record labels ready for pressing.

This new negative master is washed to remove all traces of silver picked up from the original master, then placed in another electrolytic bath to grow a further nickel coating. By using a special separating substance, this second layer of nickel can be prised away from the first, so providing a 'positive' nickel replica of the original master. The negative half is stored—it will be used to produce more positives later. Meanwhile the positive half goes back into the bath to grow another negative shell which on separation will be the stamper or 'matrix' from which copies of the final disc can be pressed in quantity. It takes two of these stampers to make a record, of course—one for each side of the disc.

Now comes the crucial moment when the 'hole in the middle' is made. An optical centring device places the hole in the exact centre of each of the stampers, working to an accuracy of 0·05 of a millimetre to ensure that the groove stays in its correct position when it revolves around the spindle of your record player at home.

The stampers will be used eventually to press out records by the thousand, but first a few test pressings are made on a hand-operated machine—the equivalent of proofs in printing. These are checked for quality before the production run begins.

Once the test pressings are approved the stampers are sent to the pressing department, where they are fixed into positions facing each other on a large automatic hydraulic press. At the touch of a button, this machine delivers the correct amount of vinyl-based material for the record, sandwiches it between two pre-printed labels, and presses them together between the stampers at a pressure of 1·575 kg per square mm and a temperature of 160°C. Seconds later, the stampers are cooled and separated to reveal the newly-pressed disc, which is then automatically—and gently—stacked on a pile at the end of the machine. Some machines sleeve the record as well. The whole process takes less than half a minute for an LP record, and less than fifteen seconds for a 17 centimetre single.

At EMI they have 120 of these presses producing up to a quarter of a million discs a day, and it's estimated that the world's 5,000 or so record companies produce a total of well over a thousand million discs a year altogether.

Snap Happy

by John Sanders

How would you like a special position at a pop concert, motor race or fashion show so that you had a clear view of everything and a chance to meet the star performers afterwards? And would you like to be paid for doing it? You would—then all you have to do is become a successful professional photographer, although this could also involve you in slightly more dangerous or uncomfortable activities like free fall parachuting with a helmet-mounted camera, covering real wars in which people shoot real bullets at you, or standing around in the cold and rain for hours waiting for some famous personality to emerge briefly from behind a closed door and confront your flash gun.

These are some of the assignments faced by photojournalists, and although film and television cameramen now provide the most immediate pictures of important news events, still photography remains a fascinating occupation that attracts many young people as their first choice of a career, especially as it is one in which anyone can succeed—regardless of race or sex—providing they have sufficient ability and determination.

Even if you don't have a burning ambition to become a well-known press, advertising, industrial or fashion photographer, owning and using a camera is a lot of fun. As with any hobby, the more you learn about it, the better it becomes and because most inexpensive modern cameras are very simple to operate, you can concentrate on getting good pictures and not worry too much about the technicalities—at least in the early stages of your new-found interest in photography.

Instant picture making, that is being able to aim a camera, press the shutter release button, have a print pop out and then watch it develop into a full colour image of what you saw within seconds, is something most people take for granted these days. But the strange fact is that although the first cameras were invented sometime back in the 11th century, it was hundreds of years before anyone could invent even a black and white film to go in them. Instead, the early photographers had to get *inside* their cameras and use their eyes to register the image it created for them—even if this was upside down.

The word camera comes from the Italian, *camera obscura*, which means darkened room and that is, quite literally, what these early cameras were—darkened rooms with a little hole in one wall through which an upside-down image of the world outside was projected on to a facing wall. Experiments with primitive lenses to sharpen the projected image were of great benefit to artists and soon portable camera obscuras in the form of tents or special carts were made so that lazy artists could travel to the scene they wished to paint and simply trace their subject on a glass screen.

A very early photograph (1835) of a window.

So beautiful were these projected images, so much clearer and full of detail than anything that even the most painstaking artist could achieve by hand, that every means was tried to fix them permanently. But alas, once the hole in the wall was covered up or the sun disappeared over the horizon, the image in the camera obscura disappeared along with it and it began to seem that photography, 'drawing with light', was no more than an impossible dream. The word, incidentally, was coined by the famous astronomer, Sir John Herschel, from two Greek words, *photos* (light) and *graphein* (to draw).

Thanks to the efforts and experiments of people like William Henry Fox Talbot and the Frenchman Joseph Nicéphore Niepce, it became possible to make permanent photographic prints using specially prepared paper and glass plates. The idea of using a flexible film base came later and although a clever American inventor, George Eastman, did not hit upon this all by himself, he did think up the word 'Kodak' to use as a trade name for his new product—and photography for everyone was just around the corner.

Loading and unloading the camera was always considered a tricky task and many people were reluctant to do it themselves. To overcome this barrier, the Kodak company invented the Instamatic, a modern version of the old box camera. To load it, all you have to do is snap in a film cartridge and it is immediately ready to take pictures. Millions of these cartridge cameras have now been made and sold and although expensive versions are available with superb interchangeable lenses and automatic exposure control over a full range of shutter speeds, these handy little pocket cameras are really designed for the snapshooter, the person who simply wants an image of a person or place with a minimum of fuss. Even the cheapest cartridge cameras virtually guarantee a recognisable result and are a marvellous way of starting photography—but these results are limited so, if you want to take the sort of pictures that you see in books and magazines, you have to be prepared to learn what makes a camera work.

Film speed

This entirely depends on the film you put in it, so let's consider the film first. No matter whether you use black and white negative film for black and white prints, colour negative film for colour prints, or transparency film for colour slides to project on a screen, the first thing you have to know is the film speed. Most film cartridges are designed to tell this to Instamatic type cameras automatically, but nearly all other cameras have to be set to the correct film speed before they

can work out the correct exposure. If you have a non-automatic camera, you have to do this by yourself and if you don't know the speed of your film, this is a sum that neither you nor your camera can even begin to work out.

Film speed is a measure of the sensitivity of the film to light. In Britain and America, this is given as an ASA rating and, in Germany, as a DIN number. Both are printed on the film pack and both add up to approximately the same exposure values for any given type of film. So with any cameras other than self-setting Instamatics or Polaroids, the first thing you must remember to do with any camera after loading it, is to set it to the film speed marked on the film container.

When a flash of light falls on a piece of film after passing through a correctly focused lens, it creates a latent image that will be made visible and permanent by developing in various chemicals. The dictionary definition of the word latent is 'hidden or concealed' and if you open the back of your camera and flood the film with light before development, any pictures you may have taken on it will vanish forever.

It has been known for thousands of years that some things are changed by exposure to light (apples are one example) but, from the very beginning, photography has depended on silver which changes very rapidly upon exposure. This is the common element in all photographic chemistry and since silver is a very uncommon metal that is becoming even more expensive and in short supply, great efforts are being made to find a suitable alternative. In the world of the future, cameras and films, as we know them today, will no doubt be museum pieces.

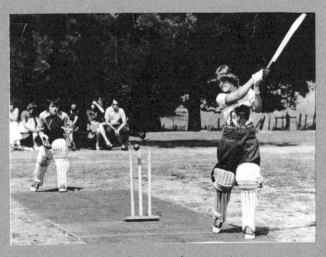

A very fast shutter speed captures the moment.

The basic parts of a camera

Since cameras are light-gathering devices, all of them have the same basic parts. These consist of a lightproof box to contain the film, a lens to collect and focus the light, a lens opening (or aperture control) to regulate the intensity of the light reaching the film, a shutter to control the length of time that light is allowed into the camera, a wind-on movement to advance the film for the next exposure and a viewfinder to tell you what the camera is 'seeing' and help you compose the picture. The aperture control also regulates the depth of focus of your picture. A portrait, for example, looks much better if the smiling face on your print is in sharp focus against an out of focus background. If everything was in sharp focus, the picture would be too busy and confusing. Your eyes are constantly selecting the things you wish them to focus on but a camera has to be told and the aperture and focus controls on your camera are the means by which you give it your instructions.

How the lens works

The difficulty of writing about a subject like photography is trying to avoid making it seem too difficult or complicated. So one way of explaining how the lens opening and shutter blades work together is to ask you to imagine the light entering the camera as a stick of Blackpool rock. If your picture is to be correctly exposed, the film must only be allowed to absorb a certain amount of it and, since the aperture also controls the depth of focus, this means using the shutter to chop off just the right length of a given thickness. A long thin bit of rock would weigh just the same as a short fat piece, and if we think of it again as light, both would expose the film correctly as regards colour and shades of grey. Pictures taken at different apertures and at correspondingly different shutter speeds do, however, look very different. A racing car taken at a slow shutter

speed would, for example, come out as a blur, while a faster shutter speed would freeze it on the track—even if it was moving at a hundred miles an hour. But, providing the lens aperture had been made larger or smaller to match the shutter speeds selected, both pictures would be correctly exposed.

There are basically three types of cameras. We call any camera 'simple' that does not offer a wide range of adjustments and is factory focused for normal picture taking from a few metres to the far horizon, or infinity. Adjustable cameras allow you to take pictures under a much wider range of conditions. The lens openings are usually designated by f-numbers and, on medium priced cameras, these would range from f/2.8 to the smallest openings of f/22. Automatic cameras combine the easy operation of a simple camera with the picture making versatility of an adjustable camera. Some have an automatic exposure control system that regulates the lens opening or shutter speed or both and on others you set the correct subject distance only. The other thing you have to remember about cameras is that they take different sizes of film. Instamatics take 110 and 126 cartridges, 35mm cameras take 135 magazines or cassettes and roll films are designated by such numbers as 127, 120 and 620. The right film has to go into the right camera or it will not work. But within these different formats, there are other variations such as the number of possible exposures you can get from them in black and white or in colour negative or transparency form.

Taking a photograph is only half the fun of making a picture. The real enjoyment of photography begins in the darkroom and although developing a film and making prints from it may seem very difficult and complicated, processing has never been so simple as it is today, even if you wish to start making prints in colour. Although many amateur photographers start straight off on colour these days, the best and cheapest way of learning about developing and printing is still to use black and white film at first. All you need for developing is a developing tank, a spiral, a measuring jug, a bottle of developer and a bottle of fixing solution. For contact printing you will need a safelight, photographic paper, a sheet of glass, a 15 watt bulb, fixing solution and some blotting paper. See the step-by-step diagrams for instructions.

You may feel that the more advanced aspects

of photography require a lot of expensive equipment but by way of encouragement perhaps I can close by telling the story of what happened when a lady wrote to the Editor of a newspaper complaining that amateur photographers did not stand a chance against professionals who used cameras worth hundreds of pounds to take their pictures.

The Editor replied by inviting the lady to his office where he presented her with the most inexpensive Instamatic camera on the market. At the same time, he introduced her to his chief photographer to whom he also handed a similar camera. He then sent them both out to take pictures at a zoo and published the results side by side in his newspaper.

The pictures taken by the lady were quite good, in the sense that most of them were sharp and a recognisable record of her outing. The pictures by the professional were, however, eye catching and powerfully composed photographs that conjured up all the menace of the tigers, the size of the elephants, and the playfulness of the chimps—rather then mere snapshots that just happened to have been taken at a zoo.

Afterwards, the lady ruefully confessed that she now realised that the skill and imagination of the person behind the camera was a far more important aspect of good picture making than the cost of the camera itself or how many different gadgets it had on it. By choosing the best position from which to photograph his subject, getting in as close as he could to it, considering the play of light and waiting until it made some active movement or the onlookers reacted to it, the professional had captured a series of decisive moments within the limitations of his inexpensive camera and had not even attempted shots that would only have been possible with a telephoto lens.

Superb equipment is not everything!

SEVEN TIPS FOR SUCCESSFUL SNAPS

1 Hold the camera level to prevent people or buildings leaning over and hold it **very** steady when you **gently** squeeze the shutter release. More blurred or unsharp pictures are caused by camera shake than any other reason.

2 Get in close and fill the viewfinder. Most amateur photographers stand much too far away from the subjects, and your friends will want to see themselves in your pictures in reasonable close-up and not as tiny figures in the far distance.

3 Find the best position. The right camera angle can make all the difference to an interesting building and, if the sun is shining, don't make human subjects squint right into it. Unless, of course, you want them to pull funny faces at you.

4 Keep the camera lens clean with a soft cloth. Fingermarked lenses produce soft, fuzzy looking pictures.

5 Add depth to your photographs by introducing some foreground such as flowers, an archway or a spray of leaves. The composition of your print or colour slide will seem much more attractive.

6 When photographing people, especially relatives and friends, don't pose them in a stiff, artificial looking group. Get them to relax and talk naturally together. One trick is to pretend you have taken the picture and then, as they all breathe sighs of relief, press the button. They will come out looking like people and not realistic waxworks.

7 Keep your pictures simple with preferably only one centre of interest and remember that a good subject is whatever you think it is—even if unusual. But even the most ordinary things or objects can be the subject of striking photographs if looked at with a little imagination.

DEVELOPING BLACK AND WHITE FILMS

1 Make up the developer and fixer according to the maker's instructions and keep in separate, labelled bottles.

2 **In complete darkness** (in a cupboard or under the stairs) wind the film on to a spiral and place it in the tank. The tank's lid must be fitted before turning the light on again.

3 Add tap water to the developer in a measuring jug, check that it is at a temperature of approximately 20°C (68°F) and pour it into the tank.

4 Agitate the developer according to the instructions you got with your tank.

5 After 3½–6 minutes (depending on the type of film), wash out the tank with plain water and immediately pour in the fix. Remember, the film will continue developing—even in plain water—until you pour in the fixing solution, so don't waste any time at this stage. (Professionals use a stop bath before pouring in the fix but this is not essential.)

6 Fix for 5–10 minutes. Insufficient fixing will leave you with a cloudy looking film so, if in doubt, leave it in the tank for an extra minute or so.

7 Pour away the fixer and wash the film in the tank in running water from the cold tap for 30 minutes. A force film washer (a short length of rubber hose and special plastic pipe which fits down into the spiral) will ensure that all the remaining chemicals are washed clean away.

8 Take out the processed film and hang it up to dry with nothing touching it. An upstairs doorway is a good place. Use a drawing pin at the top and clip a clothes peg to the bottom to prevent it curling. Avoid dust

reaching the damp film and when the negatives are dry, cut them up and store them safely in a glacine paper envelope.

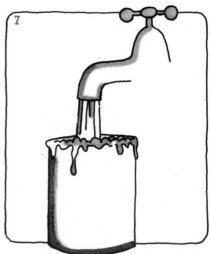

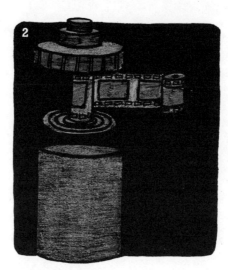

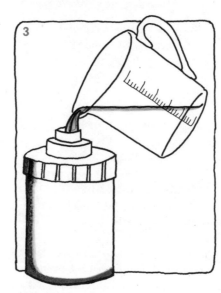

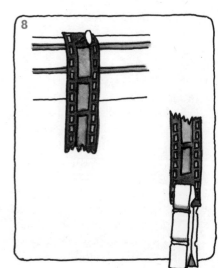

CONTACT PRINTING

1 Make sure your room is light-tight and turn off all lights except a photographic safelight. Take out one piece of photographic paper and place it smooth-side-up on a table.

2 On this place your negative(s) so that their dull side (the emulsion side) is downwards.

3 Cover them with a sheet of glass and expose them to light from a 15 watt bulb placed a metre or so away for about ten seconds.

4 Place the paper in a developing dish for about two minutes.

5 Remove, holding the paper by one corner to let the developer drain away.

6 Slide the print into a dish of fixing solution for about five minutes. You can now turn on the lights once more.

7 Wash the print in running water for 30 minutes.

8 Dry the print by sandwiching it between clean blotting paper or by hanging it up by one corner with a clothes peg.

9 Throw away all used chemicals and clean up thoroughly.

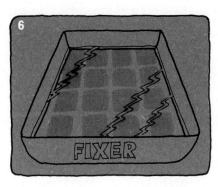

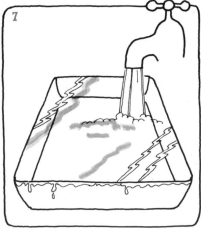

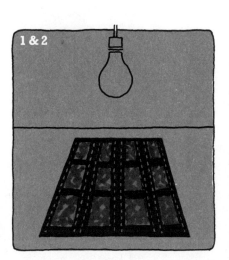

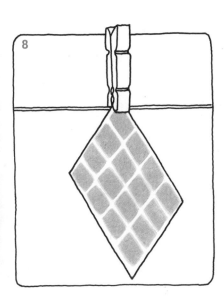

ELOCUTION CLASS

MADDOCKS.

I'D BETTER TAKE DAD FIRST!

DENTAL SURGERY

PETER—WHY AREN'T YOU IN YOUR NICE NEW WATER BED?

MADDOCKS

THE END OF THE WORLD TODAY

... FIVE, FOUR, THREE, TWO ...

"HOW ABOUT OIL OR... LIQUID FERTILIZER?"

"EXCUSE ME MRS HOUDINI — YOUR SON HAS ESCAPED FROM HIS HARNESS AGAIN!"

Drawings That Come to Life

by Terry Dixon

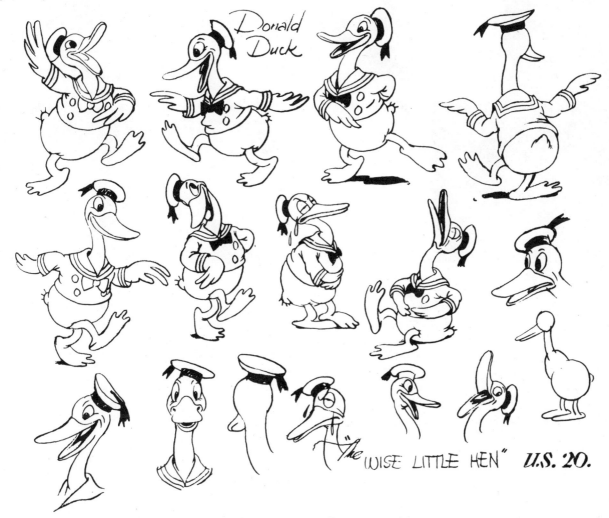

Animation—the art of making drawings appear to move—works in the same way that film itself does. All film is simply a series of photographs (stills) which, when run at the right speed on a projector, *seems* to move. The secret is in our eyes themselves and is called *image retention*. All this means is that every image our eyes see remains in our 'mind's eye' for a split second after it has gone. As we watch a screen, therefore, each still image merges with the one before and after as the film rolls and we experience the *illusion* of continuous movement. Once we know this, we can see easily that still illustrations, properly organised, can appear to have movement and life.

Walt Disney was one of the pioneers of the film cartoon. He started in 1920 and today his studio remains the biggest and best animation organisation in the world. Disney was the most important man in his field by the early 1930s and the techniques developed over the years are still used today.

A full-length Disney cartoon takes about four years to complete. The preparation involves over a hundred people and literally millions of drawings. On the screen itself you will see up to a quarter of a million hand-painted pictures.

Once an appropriate story has been decided upon and the characters designed, the first stage of

1 Character design

2 A storyboard meeting

3 An example of a storyboard

5 Xeroxing a drawing on to a cell

6 Hand painting a cell

7 Placing a cell over the background

production is to come up with a *storyboard* for each scene. This gives a good idea of how the sequence could be staged, where it might be set, whether to have close-ups or long-shots on particular lines of dialogue and so on.

After the sequence and the script have been approved at this stage, it is usual for the dialogue to be recorded by the actor who will 'play' the part so that the animators can do the final drawings to match. The animators are the heart of the production team. They are responsible for drawing the characters we actually see on the screen. They compare themselves to actors in the sense that they are creating a performance with their pencils. They also compete for the best parts in the same way that actors often do. At Disney, most animators prefer to do the comic or villainous characters such as the Dwarfs or the Wicked Witch rather than straightforward human characters such as Snow White or Prince Charming. This is obviously because they are more fun, even though the human characters are harder to draw and more difficult to make convincing.

For the characters to move and appear to have life, between twelve and twenty-five drawings of them are needed for every second of screen time. The animators, however, draw only a half to a third of this number. Also, as you can see from the photographs, they tend to draw the characters rather roughly and with lots of imprecise edges. This is because they are concerned with getting the most effective sense of movement and

with the personality of the character which is easier to capture in this way rather than being concerned with clear and precise draughtsmanship at this stage.

To finalise the drawings, therefore, several more stages are needed. First of all, the animators' work goes to the *clean-up* department where they are literally cleaned up until they consist of a clear, single pencil line. Since several animators will do the same character in different scenes, it is here in the cleaning up process that individual differences are removed so that the characters always look the same in the final film. To make sure of this *model sheets* are always produced as a firm guide. The drawings now move on again to a department where junior animators known, not surprisingly, as *in-betweeners* do the drawings in between those that the animator has done. This ensures that the broad outline of movement decided upon by the animator will be smooth and convincing when filmed.

It is not even these drawings, however, that are finally filmed. They have to be transferred to a large piece of celluloid—a cell—beforehand. This is because it would be almost impossible to re-draw the whole setting and background of a scene as well as all the characters appearing in it who are, as we have seen, re-drawn hundreds of times so that they appear to move. Instead, the background is done separately and the changes in the character are executed on the cells which are then placed over the same background.

In the old days, scores of people called ink-tracers

4 An animator at work

8 Filming cells

9 The end result

used to trace the drawings on to cells by hand. This was very laborious, time-consuming and expensive and so the Disney studio devised a process whereby the drawing is photocopied on to the cell. This takes just a few seconds instead of several minutes. If you multiply this difference by the hundreds of thousands of times the job has to be done, you can see that it is a considerable saving.

The drawing thus transferred to the cell is just an outline and so it still has to be coloured. There is no way a machine can do this: the human hand is the only answer. The Walt Disney studio has its own paint shop which makes up the paint from raw pigments; they have to control the colours exactly so that they remain constant throughout the production. For each film a special set of colours is produced. Detailed instruction charts are drawn up so that the painters always use the right colour for the right part of the right character.

By this time, the backgrounds will have been prepared and the soundtrack finalised. A very detailed schedule is drawn up for the camera operator so that the film can now be shot, frame by frame. There are twenty-five frames for every second of screen time so there is a great number of individual pictures to take. All this is done in the Camera Room. The camera is fixed, pointing downwards and anything up to five cells are placed over the appropriate background to each frame. A frame is filmed, the camera advances one frame, the operator sets up for the next frame and so on. When all these single frames are shot and the

film is run at twenty-five frames per second, finally the characters come alive!

Although the Walt Disney studio spends millions of pounds on each of their cartoons, it is quite possible to have great fun with animation for practically nothing. Walt Disney himself started nearly sixty years ago with little cut-out figures, hinged with pins at their joints so that they could be moved into different positions without having to re-draw them each time. If you can, through your family, your friends or your school, get hold of a cine camera (the simplest and cheapest will do) then you can do the same.

The easiest way of all is to use thick, black paper and cut out silhouette-like figures. Place the figures on a white background. Fix the camera and the background very firmly and shoot frame by frame, moving the characters a little bit between each shot. The illustrations, which you can trace or copy, will give you an idea of the right amount of movement, frame to frame. Don't forget, of course, that you can deliberately speed up, slow down or make your figures do the impossible. In fact, the fun of animation is that anything is possible.

If you can't get anyone to help you with a cine camera, you can much more easily make what is known as a flick book. For a flick book you will need 20 pieces of paper all the same size. If you want to animate a little man and make him walk, you have to draw him the same size 20 times. Each time his legs and arms should change positions slightly. Our series of drawings below shows you how to do this.

You can cut out these drawings and staple them together along the left hand edge to make a book. Now flick through the pages and you will see that he appears to walk. If you don't want to spoil your Mighty Magpie book, you can draw the pictures for yourself or trace them off. Of course you can draw a completely different sequence of pictures if you like.

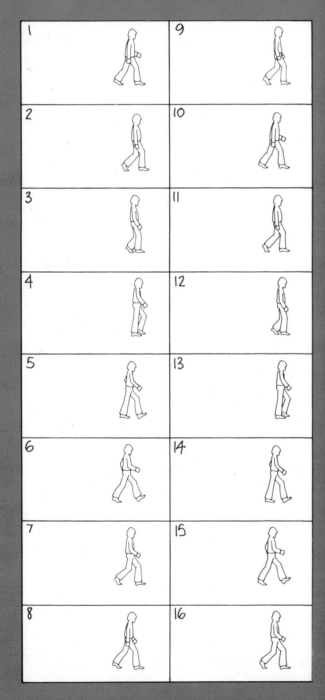

Right: A film strip of Mickey Mouse
© *Walt Disney Productions*

IT'S ANYTHING BUT A DRAG!

by Kate Marlow

Any enthusiast will tell you that this is the most straightforward of all motor sports. After all, the competitor's aim is so simple. All he hopes to do is: 'fire up his digger', 'burn out' his 'slicks', watch the 'Christmas tree', but must not 'pull a cherry', or, even worse, 'lunch his motor', before successfully 'blowing his doors off', and safely 'dropping his laundry'. What could be easier?

Just a few of the weird and wonderful machines which can be admired at a Drag Race meeting are seen here at the Santa Pod Raceway, Britain's first Drag Strip.

The motor sport is Drag Racing, America's most popular, and biggest motor sport, now enjoying great popularity over this side of the Atlantic.

Drag Racing was born in America in the early 1950s. Teenagers could be seen in their 'Hot Rods', which were hotted-up saloon cars, enjoying Traffic Light Grand Prix. The principle was simple. The first of two Hot Rods to power away the moment the lights turned to green, and pass a pre-designated point, was the victor.

The long, straight, American roads were perfect for this new 'sport', that is, until the police mounted a campaign to remove this new 'hazard' from the streets. But this was too good a thing to be allowed to die, so the competitions moved from the highways to airstrips, where two speed-merchants could race against each other and the clock, over a soon to be regularised distance of a quarter of a mile.

Crowds gathered to watch the races, which originally had a flag-start, and were timed on any available stop-watch.

Speed was, and still is, the only important factor, so anything which did not serve to increase it was removed! All but the driver's seat had to go, likewise any unnecessary cockpit fittings, and the biggest possible engine was installed. Specially-built cars which looked more like flying bedsteads with all unnecessary body-panelling removed, were soon roaring down the now named Drag 'Strips'.

The sport has escalated to amazing popularity in the States, topping Formula 1, with over 400 sanctioned strips today. These are now operated with sophisticated electronic starting and timing devices, and offer a Class for almost every type of vehicle, from 6m (20ft) long, exotic looking, purpose built machines, to ordinary saloon-type cars.

In the early 1960s, American teams came to Britain to give demonstration meetings, known as Drag Fests, at Blackbush Airfield in Hampshire. The teams included Don Garlits, the Big Daddy of Drag Racing, who is still the World Champion today. And so a new British craze was born!

In 1966 Santa Pod Raceway, Britain's first Drag Strip, was opened, on what had formerly been an airfield. Two other semi-permanent strips—Snetterton in Norfolk and Blackbush followed. Numerous airfields are also used by the National Drag Racing Club for touring meetings held across the country. A meeting has even been

held on a tarmac strip by Aintree's famous Horse Racing Course!

Crowds in excess of 60,000 have been drawn to international meetings where competitors from Germany, Holland, South Africa, Sweden and America have taken part.

Perhaps the appeal of this sport is that almost any Straight Line Racing enthusiast can acquire a car to try his hand, if he wishes. Competitors come from every walk of life, from company directors to factory workers.

It doesn't matter what class of car you race, your competitor will be evenly matched. Minis and Escorts and other ordinary saloon cars, can provide thrills, and experience for some, whilst fanatics invest in machines that cost £200 per quarter of a mile run, and which could cost a total of £8,000 if the engine should blow—or as those in the know would say, if the driver 'lunches his motor'. There are many classes in between, for both cars and motor bikes in varying stages of modification.

Dragsters, the machines from which the sport takes its name, fall into five groups, Junior, Middle, Senior, Top and Pro Fuel, with either rear

engines known as 'diggers', or front engines known as 'sling shots'.

The other real speed machines of the sport are called 'funny cars', and are wolves in sheeps' clothing. They look like any ordinary saloon car from the outside. Inside there is little but the driver's seat and controls. The body is plastic, and like the big bad dragster pro fuelers, they burn nitro methanol, and can do the quarter mile in a mere six seconds or less. Averaging well over two hundred miles per hour, they can be heard for miles around!

Funnier than the funny car is the 'wheely car', which travels the quarter reared up on its rear wheels. This spectacle is for display alone, as it is very rare for two to race, because of the high danger involved. Only two tiny stabilising wheels known as 'wheely bars' save these seemingly lunatic drivers and their machines from somersaulting backwards!

Direct competition between two drivers in each race, creates an air of high tension. Each driver must give his tyres, or 'slicks' a 'burn out' before the start. This is a process of literally burning off a layer of rubber from the tyres by spinning the wheels, and leaving this layer on the tarmac to provide a better grip for take-off. The hot tyres are reversed back over the tracks to the 'stage light'—the starting position.

The starting signal is given by electronically-operated lights known as 'Christmas trees', which show amber then green for go.

If a driver actually sees the green he knows that he was too slow off the mark, and has automatically lost his race. But a red light indicates a penalty start, known as 'pulling a cherry', which automatically disqualifies the driver. The race is timed to one thousandth of a second, from the moment an invisible beam is broken at the start, until the machine crosses the finishing line. The aim of course is to beat your opponent by crossing that line first—or to 'blow your doors off', as it's known. Pro Fuel Dragsters travelling at speeds in excess of two hundred miles an hour have to release parachutes behind them, to help them stop, hence the expression 'dropping the laundry'.

So, if you're interested, head towards the roar, fight your way through the methanol haze, and simply: 'fire your digger, burn out your slicks, watch the Christmas tree, but don't pull a cherry, and never lunch your motor, just go ahead and blow off your doors!'

MAYDAY! MAYDAY!

The story of the intrepid lifeboatmen

by Ray Kipling

Imagine a dark wintry night at the seaside with the wind howling around the chimney pots and the driving rain battering the windows of the houses. Suddenly two loud bangs interrupt the storm and green stars light up the sky. Immediately men pull on their clothes and rush down to a building right on the sea front and within minutes they're pounding through the waves in a lifeboat to go to the help of someone in trouble in a ship or a boat.

As they go out to the rescue, the lifeboatmen might be wishing they were back in their warm beds or watching the television, or they might be thinking of their wives and children. After all, they're going to help complete strangers and it's not even their full time job—they are volunteers.

The Royal National Lifeboat Institution or RNLI was formed in 1824 and is the oldest lifeboat organisation in the world. In the early days there were no engines and the boats were powered by oars and sails, they had no cabins and very little shelter and the men who formed the crews had to be fit and strong. The lifeboatmen in 1824 were volunteers, just like the men today. They all have normal daytime jobs and might be bankers, carpenters, doctors or factory workers, but they have one important thing in common—they are all good seamen. They have usually lived by the sea for a long time and so are aware of just how dangerous the sea can be.

The Legend of Grace Darling

In 1838 one of the most famous sea rescues of all time took place in an ordinary rowing boat. During a storm, the steamer Forfarshire, which was on a passage from Hull to Dundee, went aground on rocks near the Longstone lighthouse in Northumberland. The lighthouse keeper was William Darling and his daughter Grace spotted some survivors clinging to a rock. Grace and her father rowed their tiny boat through the reefs to the freezing survivors and they returned safely to the lighthouse. Grace Darling became a national heroine and a museum in Bamburgh contains her boat and many other relics of lifeboat history.

A modern day lifeboat is very different from Grace Darling's little rowing boat as it is designed specially for the purpose of sea rescues in all weathers and is fitted with the most up-to-date equipment to help with rescue operations. Lifeboats today are powered by two diesel engines and carry electrical equipment for communication and navigation. They have radios, so that they can keep in touch with people on land and with the crew of a ship in trouble, and some even have radar equipment to help them to find ships in distress. All lifeboats now have shelters where survivors may recover keeping warm with blankets and hot drinks. First aid kits are essential and a special stretcher is used to transfer injured people to the lifeboat. Searchlights, loudhailers, boathooks, scrambling nets, anchors, axes and compasses and many other items are carried as well as survival rations of biscuits, chocolate, barley sugar and brandy

The lifeboatman's equipment is very advanced too. He must keep warm and dry and so that he can be seen he wears an orange or yellow suit. The suit includes a hat so that his head is protected. His lifejacket is specially made for the RNLI and will bring his face up in the water in case he is knocked unconscious if he falls in the water. It has an orange light which is activated by sea water so that he can be seen and a whistle so that he can be heard.

The most up-to-date lifeboats are named after rivers—Clyde, Arun, Solent, Thames, Waveney and Rother. They all vary in length and most of them are designed so that they will right themselves in the water should they capsize or sink. Different sorts of lifeboats are needed because the RNLI operates lifeboats throughout the British Isles and as you can imagine, the coastline is very varied. In some places there are high cliffs and rocky shores and then a slipway is needed to launch the lifeboat into deep water. Elsewhere there might be a harbour where the lifeboat can stay afloat all the time, fixed to a mooring. In other places the harbour dries out at low tide and the lifeboat sits on a carriage which is pushed into the water by a specially waterproofed tractor. Finally there are a few beaches where the shape changes constantly as the sea moves the sand and the rocks and here the lifeboats have to be launched over greased planks of wood, or skids which can be rearranged for each launch.

More and more calls are made on lifeboats each year and hundreds of lives are saved. But with thousands of holiday-makers visiting the coast each year and going swimming, yachting, fishing or using motor boats, the lifeboatmen found that a lot of their calls were quite close to the shore, so just over ten years ago the RNLI introduced inshore lifeboats. These are small inflatable dinghies with outboard engines and are faster than the bigger lifeboats. The crews of these boats are fit young men who are prepared to be bounced around in the driving salt spray.

Bev Brown and Robin Middleton are two of the inshore lifeboat crew at New Brighton, Merseyside and they were called out just before midnight on one occasion to help a fishing boat that was in trouble. Because of the rough seas they took a crew of five men and reached the fishing boat in ten minutes to find it was aground on a sandbank. As the lifeboatmen were preparing to rescue the fishermen the fishing boat's anchor cable broke and Bev Brown realised that the boat would soon be pounded to pieces by the waves. He drove the lifeboat at full speed and rode onto the deck of the fishing boat on top of a large wave. Two men were snatched off to the safety of the lifeboat, but another man was still on board the fishing boat. Robin Middleton jumped on to the fishing boat and clambered through the loose ropes and nets to drag the injured man across to the lifeboat. They turned for home and landed the survivors who were taken away in an ambulance. It was only the superb teamwork and skill of the crew that saved the fishermen, and for their bravery Bev and Robin were awarded the RNLI's silver medal—a very high honour.

The coastguards are the men who usually spot boats in difficulty, they see the distress flares or pick up radio messages asking for help. Members of the public who see trouble at sea should inform the coastguards by telephoning 999 so that they can start the rescue operation. Maroons, which are rather like special fireworks, are used to call out the lifeboat crews. As soon as the maroon is fired the lifeboatmen drop whatever they are doing and rush to the lifeboat—every second is vital when there's a ship in trouble. Other ships at sea can often help and the coastguard might also ask for a helicopter's assistance if there's one based nearby. Helicopters

are faster than lifeboats, but they are a lot more expensive to use and can't handle every type of rescue. The volunteer lifeboatmen and the helicopter crews, who are in the Royal Air Force or the Royal Navy, hold joint practices to make sure they are ready for real emergencies. It is very exciting to see a lifeboat ploughing through the waves with a helicopter winchman slowly dropping down on to the deck, but the wind can make the job very dangerous.

The strength of lifeboats has to match the fury of the seas and although most of the work may not test them to the limit, every now and then ferocious storms toss the boats around like corks. Five London policemen will always remember the day a storm like that caught them in their yacht in the English Channel. There were waves over seven metres high, and the lifeboatmen from Yarmouth, on the Isle of Wight were called out to help them. The seas were so rough that they filled the wheelhouse of the lifeboat, but the lifeboatmen pressed on through the waves and the heavy rain and spotted the yacht. The two boats plunged up and down, one towering over the other on the crest of a huge wave and the next moment wallowing in a trough below it. The only way to rescue the policemen was to get alongside their yacht. Dave Kennett, the coxswain of the lifeboat, knew that a mistake could mean crushing a man between the two boats. Using his superb skill he picked his moment, drove the lifeboat close to the yacht and his crew snatched off three policemen. The lifeboat closed in again and the other two men were grabbed, but one, whose lifeline was attached to the yacht, fell between the two vessels. One of the lifeboatmen immediately cut through the lifeline and with a tremendous effort hauled the survivor to safety. The long journey back to the lifeboat station took nearly three hours and the lifeboatmen said they had never been out in worse weather conditions. The rescue was voted the bravest of the year and Coxswain Kennett won a silver medal. Without his great courage, seamanship and leadership the policemen would certainly have perished.

It costs a great deal of money to build lifeboats and to keep them serviced and repaired. The total cost of running the RNLI is over £5½ million each year and this is all raised by voluntary subscriptions and donations. It is comforting to know that there are men all around our coasts ready to help anyone in trouble at sea, day or night, summer or winter, calm or storm and the lifeboatmen certainly deserve our support because they're prepared to risk their lives to save others in distress, and they do it voluntarily.

Painted Ladies and Red Admirals!

by Valerie Brown

A Swallowtail, usually found in Norfolk and Cambridgeshire

Painted Lady and Red Admiral are just two of the pretty names we give to the butterflies we find in our gardens. Butterflies and moths are closely related cousins and belong to the large group of animals called Insects; they have three pairs of legs, a skin which acts like a skeleton and two pairs of large wings covered in minute scales. Each of these scales is coloured, and in the butterflies in particular the many thousands of scales on the wings can produce bright colours of red, orange, yellow and vivid blue, and striking patterns as well. But these scales are very delicate and rub off easily, which is why the colours on butterfly wings fade if you pick them up too many times.

Being cousins, butterflies and moths are very similar, but there are some differences: most butterflies have a small club on the end of their thin feelers or antennae, whereas moths do not; both have hairy bodies but in butterflies the body is usually more slender; all butterflies fly during the day but most moths fly at night.

Butterflies feed on the nectar produced by flowers, in fact they are very important pollinators of plants because while they are feeding they pick up pollen grains from one flower and take them on to the next one. They recognise the flowers they like by their colour and the patterns on their petals, and they have two large eyes, one on each side of the head, composed of several thousand individual eyes. This means that they can see in all directions at once, which is why they are so difficult to catch! Funnily enough some butterflies can taste through sense organs in their feet, so if they are put on cotton wool moistened with a solution of sugar in water they will immediately start to feed by sucking up the liquid through their long tongue. This is normally used for pushing down into the bottom of a flower, and when not in use it is kept coiled up like a watch spring under the butterfly's chin.

People who study insects are called Entomologists; those who study butterflies and moths are called Lepidopterists. Some people just collect butterflies, kill them and pin them out in boxes to make attractive displays. Others try to learn more about these delightful insects—their life histories, which flowers they visit, what their caterpillars eat and when and where to find them.

A selection of common British butterflies

Red Admiral

Peacock

Meadow Brown

Where do you find British butterflies?

There are 55 species of butterfly which are resident and breed in the British Isles, and surprisingly half of these are to be found within 25 miles of London. In addition some species, which migrate many hundreds of miles, come here for the summer; a few of these, like the Red Admiral, the Clouded Yellow and the Painted Lady, are quite common especially in years when the weather conditions are good for migration.

Our own native butterflies are not all common, and many only occur in certain parts of the country. This is because each species has its own particular preferences —its food plant must obviously be available, and the surroundings must suit all stages of the life cycle. A species which is very common over a wide area of the country is the Small Tortoiseshell, its caterpillars feed on nettles. On the other hand the Chalk-Hill Blue is only found on certain chalk and limestone hills in southern England, and then only where its food plant, the horse-shoe vetch, grows.

How to attract butterflies to your garden

Since butterflies are among Britain's most beautiful insects, it is very satisfying to see them in your garden, and many people endeavour to attract them. Butterflies feed on the sugary nectar of flowers, so flowers which produce an abundance of nectar are likely to lure a wide range of butterfly species. These flowers usually have a strong, sweet scent which advertises their nectar. The flowers associated with an old English country garden, such as daisies, sweet rocket, golden rod, valerian and buddleia, are preferred to the more exotic roses, gladioli or chrysanthemums. Rotting fruit, though undesirable in your garden, attracts several butterflies, for instance the Red Admiral.

As well as feeding, the female butterfly will want to find a suitable plant on which to lay her eggs. Unfortunately for the keen gardener, certain weeds, such as nettles, are popular with several of our most spectacular butterflies. Butterflies will feed on a range of flowers, but their caterpillars are much more

particular. It is impossible to mention all the types of caterpillar together with their favourite food plant, but here are just a few examples:

Caterpillars of the Small Tortoiseshell, Red Admiral, Comma and Peacock feed on Stinging Nettles. The Dog Violet is the food-plant of the Dark Green Fritillary, and the low creeping Bird's-foot Trefoil and Rest Harrow for the Common Blue. The leaves of trees, such as Willow and Sallow, are eaten by the caterpillars of the Camberwell Beauty, and grasses, such as Cocksfoot, by the Speckled Wood.

Caterpillars feeding on plants eaten or used by man are regarded as pests. The food of the Large White can be any member of the cabbage family, a feature which probably makes this species the leading butterfly pest in Britain.

Life cycle

Most animals simply get larger and larger as they grow older, without changing their form dramatically. Butterflies are different; young butterflies are called caterpillars—they eat plants and cannot fly. When fully grown they change into the butterfly which we all know.

Butterflies lay their eggs on plants, but they are very careful to choose a plant which their young can eat. They usually glue their eggs to the underside of leaves so that they are protected from rain and hot sunshine, and are not easily seen by animals which like to eat them. The Large White lays clusters of eggs on the underside of cabbage leaves, and sometimes there are more than 100 eggs in each cluster.

The eggs are often bright yellow or green in colour and are filled with yolk which is eaten by the developing caterpillar as it grows inside the egg shell. When the caterpillar hatches it chews its way through the shell and often eats it.

Caterpillars are worm-like creatures with enormous appetites. They spend nearly all their time chewing the leaves of plants, and as they get older they have to shed their skin several times so that they can grow

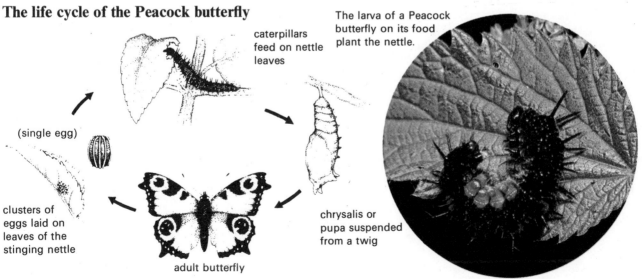

Common Blue   Orange Tip   Large Cabbage White

larger. The leaves of many of the plants in your garden probably have holes in them, which shows where caterpillars have been feeding. Even though caterpillars are very hungry animals they only eat certain plants, which they recognise by their smell, and would rather starve to death than eat anything else!

When a caterpillar is ready to change into a butterfly it crawls away to a quiet place and suspends itself from a silk pad which it spins; sometimes it also makes a silk girdle which it wraps around itself. It then sheds its skin again and changes into a pupa or chrysalis, which cannot move. The cracks in garden fences or the walls of garden sheds are favourite places for butterfly pupae. After a while the chrysalis breaks open and a fully-formed butterfly emerges. But there is one more thing it must do before it can fly—it has to unfold its crumpled wings and let them dry. Before the female butterfly can lay her eggs she must attract a mate. This she does by producing a scent which is only attractive to males of her species.

It often takes a whole year for an egg to become an adult butterfly, but some species grow faster and produce more than one generation each year.

Breeding butterflies yourself

Breeding butterflies is an absorbing hobby for which one needs only very simple equipment. The insects kept in captivity are called a 'culture', and this can be started in several different ways. You can look for eggs or caterpillars on plants, or buy a few eggs of some species from a butterfly farm. It is probably not a good idea to start by collecting adult butterflies, because you will not always know on which type of plant the caterpillars feed.

The eggs are best kept in any small tightly sealed container 5cm (2in) square so that they do not dry out; holes are unnecessary at this stage and would certainly allow the newly hatched caterpillars to escape. It is best to keep the eggs at room temperature and never in the sun. As soon as the eggs hatch the minute caterpillars should be moved to a slightly larger air-tight box containing a few leaves of the food-plant; this should be done very carefully with a small paint brush. If they are put in too large a container they will wander away from their food and quickly starve to death.

After a few days the caterpillars will shed their

The life cycle of the Peacock butterfly

caterpillars
feed on nettle
leaves

The larva of a Peacock butterfly on its food plant the nettle.

(single egg)

clusters of
eggs laid on
leaves of the
stinging nettle

chrysalis or
pupa suspended
from a twig

adult butterfly

Above: A Small Tortoiseshell on nettles.

skins for the first time. When this has happened yet again they should be moved into a larger container, such as an old shoe box, in the lid of which is cut a large hole. This hole should be covered carefully with fine nylon net, muslin or even ladies' tights.

It is very important to change the food regularly; the caterpillars will suffer badly if they do not have fresh food at all times. One way to make the food last longer is to push the plant stems into pots of damp sand; do not use water because the caterpillars will drown. As the caterpillars feed they produce droppings known as 'frass', and if these are dry pellets you can be reasonably sure that the caterpillars are healthy. The frass and any dead material should be removed each day to prevent the spread of disease. As the caterpillars grow older you will be surprised how much they eat, and you should be careful not to have too many in each cage.

When the caterpillars are fully grown they stop eating and settle down to pupate. When the last caterpillar has stopped feeding the food may be removed, and the pupae left undisturbed until the adult butterflies emerge. If this does not happen for a long time (ie during the winter) it is probably worthwhile putting some damp peat in the box. The emerging butterflies will appreciate some twigs to climb, so that they can expand their wings.

The newly emerged butterflies can be released into your garden, but **never** release foreign species or garden pests like the Large White. Releasing uncommon species into the wild can help to increase their numbers, and in this way you can play an important part in conservation.

Migration

As we have seen some butterflies spend their entire life cycle in a restricted area such as a garden. What is more, future generations will also stay in the area. However, certain species undergo mass movements to a completely different region, sometimes a different country or even continent. These movements are called migrations, and the best examples are seen in butterflies from the tropics.

A migration is a way of avoiding unfavourable conditions, such as a lack of food, extreme weather conditions, or overcrowding. The Monarch butterfly is famous for its long annual migrations. The butterfly breeds in Canada and the northern United States, but moves south to pass the winter in places like California and Mexico; during these movements some individuals even stray across the Atlantic and are occasionally found in Britain!

Camouflage and mimicry

Butterflies and caterpillars are an attractive meal for many different varieties of animal. For this reason they are often coloured to blend in with their surroundings, so that their presence is less obvious. The wings of butterflies are sometimes shaped and coloured like leaves. In most types the undersurface of the wings, which is the only part you see when a butterfly is resting, is dull in colour and patterned to resemble bark or stones.

Other butterflies are the complete opposite; they like to advertise their presence by being vividly coloured. Birds attempting to eat one of these may have a nasty shock, because they often contain chemicals which are very unpleasant to taste. This experience teaches the bird to avoid that type of butterfly in the future! So the bright colours serve as a warning to predators. Other butterflies, which would be much more pleasant to eat, copy or mimic the warning colours of the poisonous butterflies, and in this way they too are protected from predators.

Migration of the Large Cabbage White butterfly

Large migrating swarms are seen in Central Europe from June to August.

CROSSWORLD

There are 36 countries in this crossword—but you'll discover they are not in the right places!

Answers on page 128

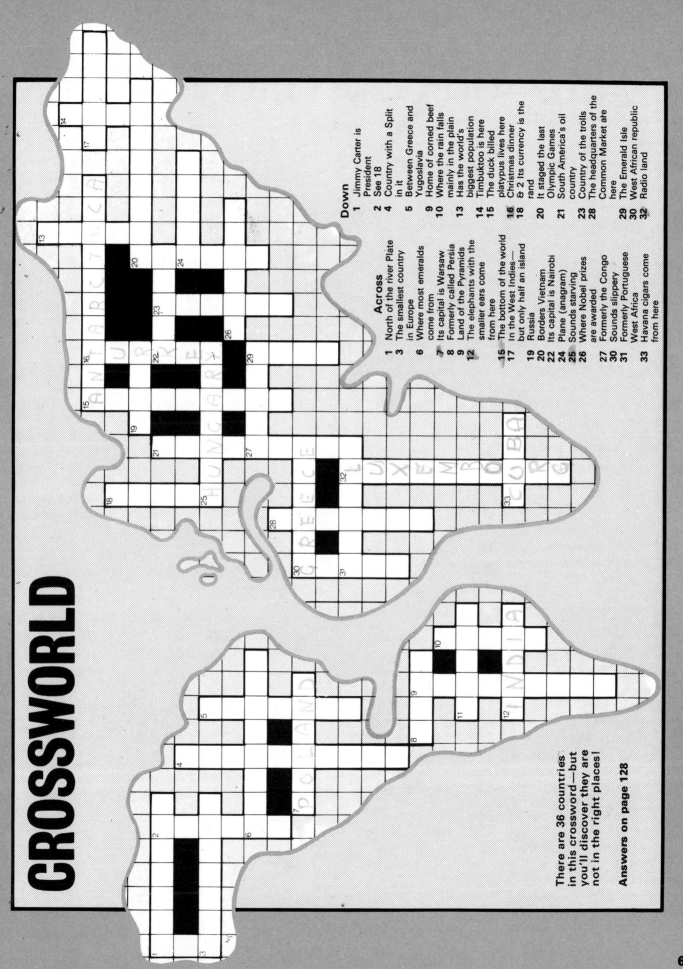

Across

1 North of the river Plate
3 The smallest country in Europe
6 Where most emeralds come from
7 Its capital is Warsaw
8 Formerly called Persia
9 Land of the Pyramids
12 The elephants with the smaller ears come from here
15 The bottom of the world
17 In the West Indies—but only half an island
19 Russia
20 Borders Vietnam
22 Its capital is Nairobi
24 Plane (anagram)
25 Sounds starving
26 Where Nobel prizes are awarded
27 Formerly the Congo
30 Sounds slippery
31 Formerly Portuguese West Africa
33 Havana cigars come from here

Down

1 Jimmy Carter is President
2 See 18
4 Country with a Split in it
5 Between Greece and Yugoslavia
9 Home of corned beef
10 Where the rain falls mainly in the plain
13 Has the world's biggest population
14 Timbuktoo is here
15 The duck billed platypus lives here
16 Christmas dinner
18 & 2 Its currency is the rand
20 It staged the last Olympic Games
21 South America's oil country
23 Country of the trolls
28 The headquarters of the Common Market are here
29 The Emerald Isle
30 West African republic
32 Radio land

65

BUILD YOUR OWN EIFFEL TOWER

by Graham Elson

You will need: A piece of plywood or chipboard measuring 26 by 66cm and at least 12mm thick; a piece of black felt 36 by 76cm; metric graph paper; a ball of Twilley's Goldfingering in silver; panel pins, 19mm long; clear household adhesive; a small block of wood 12mm thick as a depth gauge.

The design: On squared graph paper make an actual size template of the design from the diagram (each square equals 2cm) using a dot to represent each pin. Space the dots evenly in each row and mark the lines A1-A19, B1-B19 etc. You may find it helpful to use a pair of dividers to space out these pin positions, 'walking' them up and down the rows until the required number of dots are evenly spaced.

To make up the board: Cover the board with felt or alternatively, paint it matt black. If you decide to use felt, lay the board in the centre of the fabric and spread adhesive down the two long edges. Pull the felt taut and stick in place. Glue the other sides in place, mitring the corners of the felt for neatness.

Positioning the pins: Place the graph paper over the right side of the board, holding the corners in place with drawing pins. Hammer the pins in position through the paper using the depth gauge so that all the pins are the same height. Ask a parent to help with the hammering if you find it difficult. Remove the graph paper plan.

Threading the design: You may find it helpful to use tweezers to tie the knots securely. Tie to pin A1 and pass the thread round B1 to C1 then to C2 (see diagram 1a), on to B2, A2, A3 (see diagram 1b) B3, C3, C4, B4, A4 etc. Continue in this sequence to C19 and tie off.

Tie to pin D and loop round E1 to D to E2 to D to E3 to D, E4, D and tie off. Tie to F and similarly pass round G1 to F to G2, F, G3, F, G4, F, and tie off.

Tie to H1 and pass round J1, back to H1 to H2 (see diagram 2), J2, H2, H3, J3, H3, H4, J4, H4 and tie off. Similarly tie to K1, pass round L1, K1, K2, L2, K2, K3, etc.

Tie to M1, pass round N1 to O1, P1, M2, N2, O2, P2, M3 etc. Continue in this way to P11 and tie off.

Tie to Q and following diagram 3 pass around every other pin on each side of the tower. At the top, return threading the other side of the same pins (see dotted lines on diagram 3), tying off on Q. Repeat, tying on at R but do not tie off, pass the thread up the outside of the tower, over the top, just below T and down the other side, tying off on Q.

Finally tie to S and pass round each of the eleven pins in row T, returning to S each time, then loop round U, back to S and tie off.

Fix picture hangers to the back of the picture to complete.

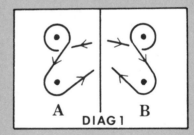

A DIAG 1 B

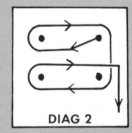

DIAG 2

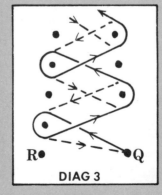

R Q

DIAG 3

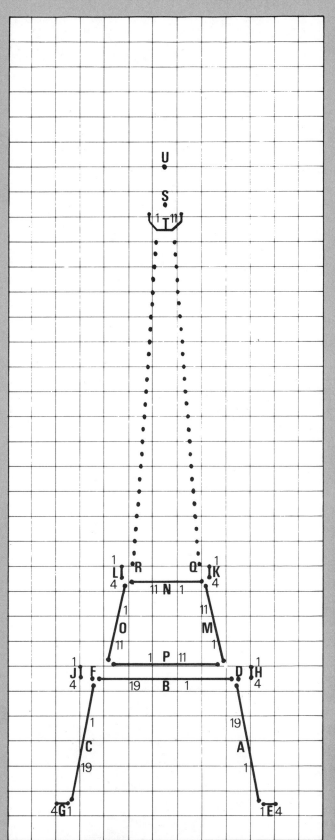

" NO SIGN OF LIFE... "

Make & Do Presents

by Danielle Sacher

GIFT TAGS

CUT OUT A PIECE OF STRONG CARD ABOUT 15 cm (6in) SQUARE. CUT OUT A SMALLER PICTURE FROM A MAGAZINE OR BOOK AND STICK IT ONTO THE CARD. BOLD SIMPLE SHAPES WORK BEST SUCH AS A FISH, A CAR, AN APPLE ETC. PUT A FEW DABS OF GLUE ON THE PICTURE AND THEN SPRINKLE ON SOME GLITTER. WHEN THIS IS DRY PUNCH A HOLE AT THE TOP OF THE CARD AND THREAD SOME PRETTY STRING OR RIBBON THROUGH THE CARD. WRITE TO... AND FROM... ON THE BACK OF THE CARD AND TIE IT ON TO THE PRESENT.

GREETING CARDS

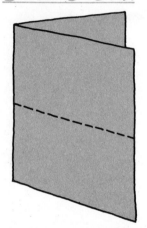
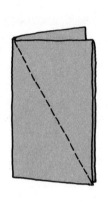

CUT OUT A PIECE OF STRONG WHITE PAPER TO FIT YOUR ENVELOPE. CUT OUT TWO PIECES OF TISSUE PAPER OF CONTRASTING COLOURS SLIGHTLY SMALLER THAN THE WHITE PAPER. FOLD THE TISSUE PAPER THREE TIMES TO MAKE A TRIANGLE, AS SHOWN IN THE DIAGRAM. CUT SMALL HOLES IN THE EDGE OF EACH PIECE OF TISSUE. OPEN UP THE PIECES OF TISSUE AND CAREFULLY GLUE THEM ONE ON TOP OF THE OTHER ONTO THE CARD USING VERY LITTLE GLUE. THE RESULT IS A PRETTY STAINED GLASS EFFECT.

SIMPLE BADGES.

STICK A PICTURE OF YOUR FAVOURITE POP STAR OR CARTOON CHARACTER ONTO A FIRM PIECE OF CARD. CUT ROUND THE SHAPE OF THE PICTURE AND THEN COVER IT WITH TWO COATS OF LACQUER. WHEN THIS IS DRY STICK A SAFETY PIN ON TO THE BACK OF THE BADGE WITH SELLOTAPE. YOUR BADGE IS NOW READY TO WEAR.

I'm a Sled Kite-Fly Me!

YOU WILL NEED : A SQUARE OF THIN PLASTIC, STICKY TAPE (OR CARPET TAPE), 2 BAMBOO OR DOWELL STICKS, A PIECE OF CHALK , A PAIR OF SCISSORS , THIN STRING

1 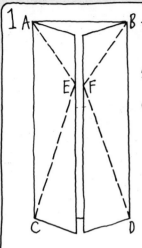 TAKE A SQUARE OF THIN PLASTIC—A PIECE FROM A RUBBISH BAG WILL DO. THE BEST SIZE IS 1m X 1m (3ft X 3ft). MEASURE OUT YOUR KITE BY FOLDING THE TWO SIDES OF THE PLASTIC SO THAT THEY MEET IN THE MIDDLE. MARK THE POINTS A TO F AND THE CUTTING LINES AS IN THE DIAGRAM.

2 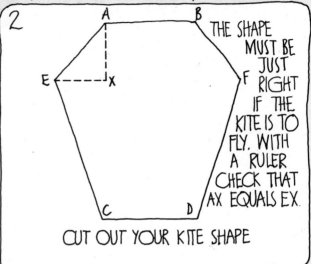 THE SHAPE MUST BE JUST RIGHT IF THE KITE IS TO FLY. WITH A RULER CHECK THAT AX EQUALS EX.

CUT OUT YOUR KITE SHAPE

3 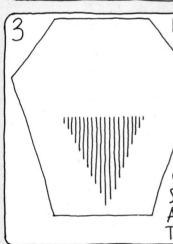 MEASURE HALF-WAY DOWN THE KITE AND IN THE BOTTOM HALF, MARK OUT AN UPSIDE-DOWN TRIANGLE . IT'S TIP SHOULD BE QUITE NEAR THE BOTTOM OF THE KITE. CUT SLITS 2.5 cm.(1 in.) APART INSIDE THE TRIANGLE.

4 TAKE TWO BAMBOO OR DOWELL STICKS AND PLACE THEM ON YOUR KITE ONE AT AC AND THE OTHER AT BD. ATTACH THEM TO THE PLASTIC WITH STICKY TAPE OR CARPET TAPE IS EVEN BETTER.

STICK TWO SQUARES OF TAPE EACH MEASURING APPROXIMATELY 7.5cm X 7.5cm (3in X 3in) AT THE POINTS E AND F. PIERCE A HOLE IN EACH OF THE SQUARES.

5 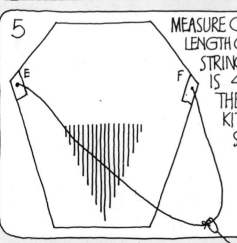 MEASURE OUT A LENGTH OF THIN STRING THAT IS 4 TIMES THE WIDTH OF THE KITE (3.5 m (12ft) FOR A 1m (3ft) KITE). THREAD IT THROUGH THE HOLES AT E AND F SECURING IT AT EACH POINT WITH A KNOT. TIE A SMALL LOOP IN THE MIDDLE OF THE STRING. (IT'S VERY IMPORTANT FOR THE LOOP TO BE EXACTLY IN THE MIDDLE.) TIE THE FLYING LINE (MADE OF THIN STRING) TO THE LOOP.

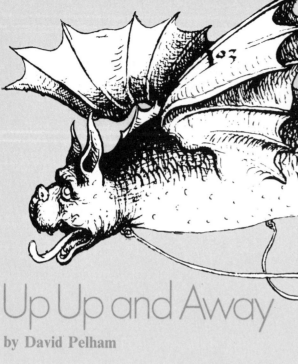

Up Up and Away

by David Pelham

The kite was first invented in China long before
the beginnings of written history. Silk was being
produced in China as early as 2600 BC and as
bamboo cane was plentiful kites were probably
being flown by the Chinese around 1000 BC.
Chinese folklore is full of stories of kites flown
both for fun and for a special purpose. One of its
more ingenious uses was demonstrated by the Han
general Han Hsin in the year 169 BC. In order to
dig a tunnel for his troops to enter under the walls
of a palace, he is said to have used a kite to gauge
the distance between his forces and the palace
walls. Chinese legend also tells us that Liu Pang,
founder of the Han Dynasty in 202 BC, was
opposed by a general Huan Theng, a fierce defender
of the previous order. Huan Theng and his army
were eventually surrounded and threatened with
death. It is said that a lucky gust of wind carried
Huan Theng's hat from his head, giving him the
idea of building a large quantity of kites fitted with
sounding devices. These would probably have
taken the form of finely-shaved bamboo strips held
taut between the ends of a bow, and were flown in
the dead of night above the army of Liu Pang, who,
on hearing the mysterious wailing in the sky,
supposedly panicked and fled.

A well-known story from Japan relates how the
famous robber Kakinoki Kinsuke used a
man-carrying kite in an attempt to steal the scales
from the golden dolphins on top of the towers of
Nagoya Castle. Fate seems to have been against

Above: A portrait of Samuel Franklin Cody and right an early
fifteenth-century kite being flown.

Text and photographs in this article are courtesy of David Pelham and are taken from The Penguin Book of Kites

Above: An early twentieth-century Chinese figure kite.

him however, for although he landed safely after successfully dislodging a number of scales, he was later arrested and punished by being boiled in oil together with his entire family.

Also in Japan, kites were used by workmen building towers to lift tiles and bricks up to them. The kites flew overhead carrying large baskets full of the materials they needed.

Certainly the most famous Japanese kite was the Wan-wan kite, developed by Nagajima Gempei around the turn of the last century. With an overall width of 24m (60ft), and a tail of 146m (480ft), it weighed approximately 2.80 tonnes (6160lb), and required a team of about 150 men to launch and fly it.

The kite was thought to be quite amazing when it was first introduced into Europe by Dutch traders in the middle of the fifteenth century, but soon kite-flying became very popular. However, it was not until the eighteenth century that the kite was really put to work by such experimenters as Benjamin Franklin. In 1752, with the aid of his son, Franklin flew his kite and proved that lightning was an electric discharge.

Benjamin Franklin also recorded how he used a kite to propel himself, whilst floating on his back, across a pond. Probably the most flamboyant use of the kite as a carriage was that devised by the English schoolteacher George Pocock, whose famous 'char-volant' was patented in 1826. Drawn by two adapted English arch top kites, Pocock's

lightweight carriage was capable of carrying four or five passengers at speeds of up to 20 miles per hour.

The earliest experiments made with the shape of the kite were those of Sir George Cayley made between 1799 and 1809. Cayley's first model glider, made in 1804, incorporated an English arch top kite as a wing unit. Had he had enough power there is little doubt that as a result of his work the aeroplane would have been invented much sooner than it was. However, in the absence of such an engine, man had to be content with the humble wind-borne kite in order to reach the clouds.

In 1893 Lawrence Hargrave invented his unique and highly efficient box kite. Like Cayley, Hargrave's experiments with the shape of the kite were a by-product of his ambitions towards powered flight. So stable was Hargrave's box kite that it was used extensively for meteorological survey well into the twentieth century, and also contributed greatly in research towards manned flight.

Among all the pioneers of early aviation, probably the most remarkable was the flamboyant Samuel Franklin Cody—a cowboy from Texas, who used a winged version of Hargrave's box kite in his man lifting system in 1901. Although he started out by raising observers on kites for the British Army, Cody went on to power his own kites, and in October 1908 he became the first man to build and fly an aeroplane in Britain.

Not all of Cody's kite experiments were made for the army however, for he did a lot of work for the meteorological office. On one occasion he raised instruments to the then record height of 4,268m or approximately 14,000ft.

On the other side of the Atlantic, man lifting was being developed by Dr Alexander Graham Bell, whose first aeronautical experiments were undertaken purely for entertainment and amusement. Gradually Dr Bell's experiments became more serious as he realized the potential of their contribution to man's conquest of the air.

Although he never succeeded, his experiments resulted in some of the most beautiful kites ever made. Pyramidal in shape and covered on two sides with silk, Bell's kites could be extended indefinitely by simply adding on more pyramids. When the Wright Brothers wanted to test their early gliders in 1902 they flew them as kites. The simple shape of the pyramid was the key which finally enabled man to develop a successful design for an aeroplane.

Eleven of the Best

Everyone knows of George Best—one of the most exciting footballers on the British football scene. But who does George regard as his personal football favourites? We asked him to tell us his all-time-great football eleven and he came up with the team you see here. World beaters? We'll never know that but we do know modest George has even given us an alternative name for the number eleven shirt!

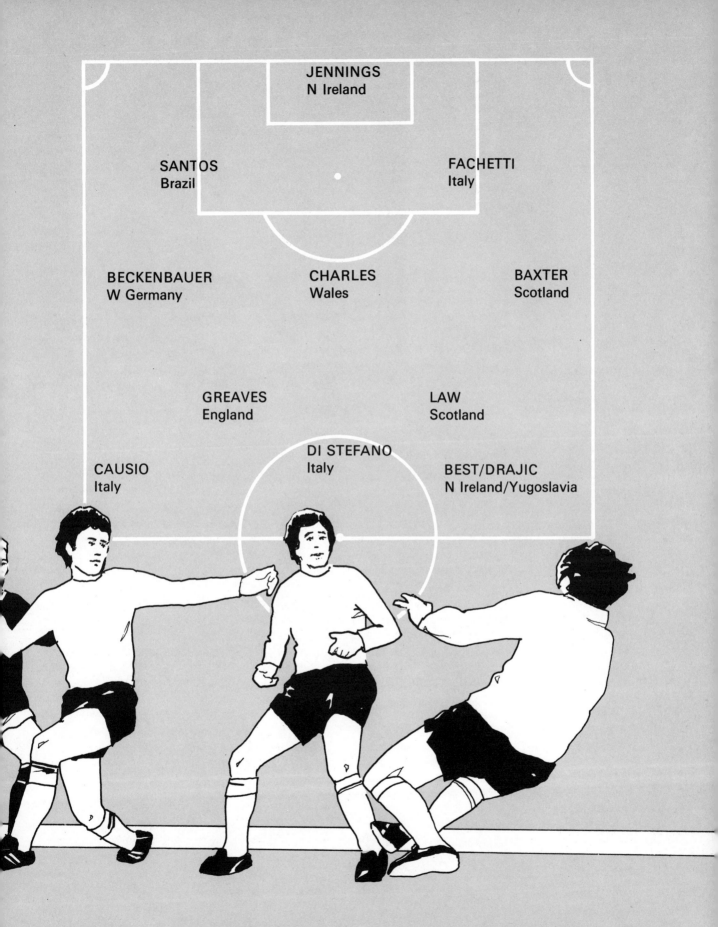

JENNINGS
N Ireland

SANTOS
Brazil

FACHETTI
Italy

BECKENBAUER
W Germany

CHARLES
Wales

BAXTER
Scotland

GREAVES
England

LAW
Scotland

DI STEFANO
Italy

CAUSIO
Italy

BEST/DRAJIC
N Ireland/Yugoslavia

Houdini

Cardini

COULD YOU BE A MAGICIAN?

by Mick Loftus

Conjuring, prestidigitation, sleight of hand—call it what you will—the art of magic has absorbed and baffled mankind for century after century. And it looks set to continue doing so for many centuries to come. For as long as the world's fifty thousand or more magicians keep inventing new tricks and illusions, they'll find millions of spectators to watch them closely and wonder how it's done. Television, itself a magical feat of electronic wizardry, has brought the magician's art to a vaster audience than was ever dreamed of by the first man to perform a trick in public. Who he was, and what he did to puzzle people, no one knows. But we can be sure that the history of magic dates back to long before the first trick was invented.

To prehistoric man, no better equipped for survival than the animals he shared the earth with, there was magic everywhere. It was in the wind and the rain, in thunder and lightning, in birth and in death, and in the countless wonders of nature. He didn't understand any of these things as we do today, and so they frightened him. This made him ripe to be preyed upon by the people who soon appeared calling themselves wizards, witches or sorcerers. These people, with their strange chants and magic potions, seemed to have direct contact with the forces of nature. They could produce fire

and rain, heal the sick, foretell the future—or so it seemed to those around them. But really they were nothing more than students of nature—the first scientists, in fact. You can see their equivalent today in the witch doctors who still hold prominent positions in the world's few remaining primitive tribes.

For centuries the wizards were all-powerful. They sat at the right hand of kings who would rather employ them than risk having them as enemies. And whatever happened, their reputations were safe. If their magic worked, it confirmed their superhuman powers. If it didn't, it could only mean that the gods were angry. By this simple reasoning, wizards kept their privileged positions. But as time went by and man's knowledge of the world increased, the sorcerers were gradually revealed as ordinary humans putting on an act. Eventually witchcraft was made a crime, and the common punishment for those who practised it was death by burning at the stake.

But not all magicians had evil ends in view. The history of magic as an *entertainment* dates back more than five thousand years, according to the ancient documents and wall paintings unearthed by archaeologists in Egypt. From then until the late sixteenth century, in England at any rate,

conjurers and magicians were little more than strolling players, vagabonds who wandered from town to town performing their sadly limited number of tricks in the streets and inns for the few coins that might be tossed their way. Then in 1582 something happened which was to set the magician's art on the road to becoming the spectacular entertainment it is today: the first book on magic appeared. It was written by Reginald Scott, a man who had never performed a trick in his life. He called his book *The Discoverie of Witchcraft*, and it revealed the secrets behind most of the magic tricks then being performed. This book, and the countless publications which followed over the next two hundred years, forced magicians to think again about their acts, and to come up with new ideas often enough to stay ahead of the reading public. On the whole they failed. But one man, a Frenchman born in 1805, introduced so many new ideas and amazed so many people in such an original new style that he came to be known as 'The Father of Modern Magic'.

His name was Jean Eugene Robert Houdin. He was a master craftsman as well as a mechanical genius, and when he decided to apply these skills to improving the often bulky stage equipment used by the magicians of the day, he created effects that would inspire performers and captivate audiences for generations to come. He used electro-magnets (a little-known invention in those days) concealed under the stage to make light objects heavy at the touch of a hidden button. He perfected the illusion known as 'levitation' in which a human subject is left suspended in mid-air with no apparent means of support. And instead of dressing in the flowing robes of a wizard, he wore elegant evening clothes and started a tradition which still survives. He travelled the world, drawing large audiences wherever he went, and before he died in 1871 he published a full account of all his methods.

About twenty years later a young would-be magician called Erich Weiss picked up a copy of Robert Houdin's memoirs in a New York second-hand shop and was so impressed by what he read that he determined to make an equally successful career for himself. He even changed his name to Houdini, which means 'like Houdin', and set out to conquer the world with his magic. He did—and became the best-known illusionist of all time. But the most famous part of his act was really no illusion at all, though no one knew it at the time. The fact was—and he proved it over and over again—that he could escape from any bondage ever devised. In minutes, and sometimes even seconds, he freed himself from Scotland Yard handcuffs, prison cells, bank safes, chained and padlocked trunks, ice-bound rivers, and even unusual things like milk churns and rolltop desks! Like his French idol, Houdini was obsessed with how things worked, particularly locks, and it was his study of their strengths and weaknesses that enabled him to perform his speedy and sensational escapes. Above all, he was a showman, as every successful magician must be, and it was this quality that made him as famous—and as well paid—as any film star.

The art of conjuring is to make things appear seemingly from nowhere, and no one did it better than a young Welsh magician who emerged just after the First World War. His real name was Pitchford, but he changed it to Cardini, since his act was concerned with playing cards which he handled with a skill that could only be compared with that of Houdini. He appeared in immaculate evening dress, complete with top hat, white gloves and monocle, and pretended to be slightly drunk. Soft music would play, and Cardini never spoke throughout his act. Suddenly a fan of cards would appear in one of his hands, and he would look as surprised as the audience. One by one, he dropped them to the floor, and as soon as the last one fluttered down, another fan appeared as mysteriously as the first. This happened several times. Then, just when the audience thought there could not possibly be any more cards, a whole pack appeared in the artist's hands. After manipulating them in a dazzling display, he squeezed them until the pack became smaller and smaller and finally disappeared, only to appear again seconds later, restored to their original size. Even more baffling was the similar routine Cardini performed with lighted cigarettes— dozens of them—which appeared and vanished so many times and in so many different combinations that the spellbound audience could only wonder how the man avoided setting his clothes on fire!

By this time The Magic Circle, the world-famous international club for magicians founded in 1905, had over 300 members. It was proving to be a useful meeting place for all who took magic seriously, whether professional or amateur. Here, they could exchange ideas and try out ambitious new tricks on people who would criticise and suggest improvements. For the first time, magicians were working together to help magic

compete with the increasingly impressive wonders of the twentieth century. Today, The Magic Circle boasts about 1500 members, and includes many famous and unexpected names in its ranks: J B Priestley, Orson Welles, David Hemmings, Lord Mountbatten and many more. Among the professionals, the two best known are probably David Nixon, rightly famous for making magic work, even under the watchful eye of television—and Tommy Cooper, equally famous for making tricks fail hilariously, an art in itself.

To qualify for membership of The Magic Circle, you must not only have a keen interest in magic, but also be able to perform a number of tricks to a very high standard. If a trick interests you, practise it over and over again until you can do it almost without thinking. Then try it on your friends. And don't forget the importance of showmanship—without it, Robert Houdin, Houdini and Cardini would never have become famous, and neither will you! If you're really keen you'll read everything you can lay your hands on about the secrets of magic and the art of performing. Your local library will almost certainly have a number of books in stock to start you off. Meanwhile, if you just can't wait to get started, here are four tricks using everyday objects you can try straight away. They're quite simple to learn, but remember: the smoother your performance, the more impressive they'll be.

★★★

The String-Band Trick

Tie the ends of a 1m (3ft) string together to form a loop. Hold it between your middle fingers as shown. Lock it in' by placing a rubber band round all four fingers. Tell the audience the string is now immobile but that you are going to move it by magic to the other two fingers. They watch you wind it round your hand. You say the magic word. Then you unwind it and—presto—the string is now on the other two fingers.

How it's done:
Take the side of the loop nearest to you and wind it over the top first, then pick up the second half as your hand goes round again. Continue winding. When you unwind, the string will be on the other two fingers. Practise this till you can do it easily and fairly swiftly for the best results.

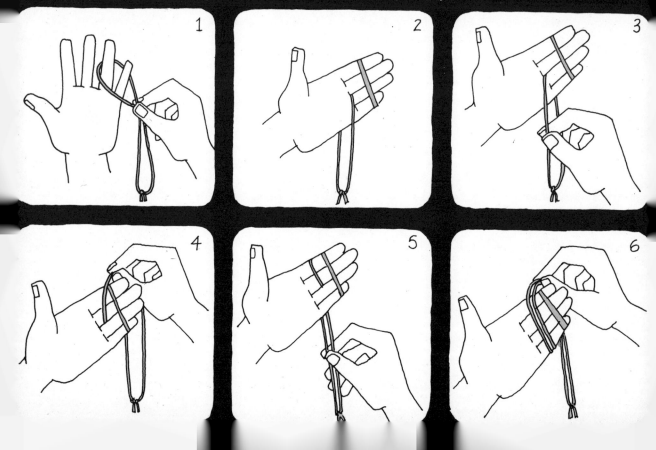

spread a square scarf or handkerchief flat on a table. Place a coin in the exact centre. Fold the scarf corner to corner, then in half again as shown, A to B. Fold in half once more, hold the scarf up by corners A, B and C and invite spectators to feel coin still in the scarf. Now, holding corners A and B between your index fingers and thumbs, stretch the scarf tight, letting go of corner C. The coin will be held in the folds as shown. To make it 'disappear' tilt the scarf until the coin rolls

towards the lower hand. Just before it arrives, release the scarf with your lower hand and catch the coin secretly. At the same time whip the scarf away sharply with your higher hand, to distract attention from the hand with the coin. Give the scarf to a spectator for examination—quietly pocket the coin while he's doing this.
Note: This trick is easy enough to learn, but needs *practice* before it can be impressive!

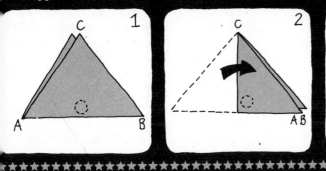

Guessing the Coin

With the secret help of a friend, you can guess the value of any coin placed under an upturned cup while you're out of the room. Before the performance, you must agree with your friend (who will place the cup over each coin given him) on a 'clock code' by which the position of the cup's handle will tell you the coin's value. A simple code might be:

2 o'clock	= $\frac{1}{2}$p
4 o'clock	= 1p
6 o'clock	= 2p
8 o'clock	= 5p
10 o'clock	= 10p
12 o'clock	= 50p

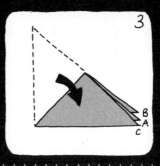

Or if you want to be more devious, you can make the positions more irregular. **Note:** Always make sure you're agreed on which way up the imaginary clock is standing, i.e., with twelve o'clock pointing to a certain corner or edge of the table.

Naming the Card

Ask a volunteer to shuffle a pack of cards, then to place the pack face down and cut them about half way. Tell him to pick up one half and count the cards. (It should come to between 21 and 29—if it doesn't, tell him to cut again nearer the middle!) Now tell him to add the two digits of the number he's counted, for example if he counted 23 cards he adds them up to five, 27 becomes nine etc. Now ask him to turn the half-pack he's just counted face-up and count off the number he's just obtained, and to memorise the last card counted. (Example: if the two digits added to six he'll remember the sixth card!) Now tell him to

put back the cards he's counted and place the half-pack he's holding face-down on the other half pack. (**Note:** So far, the volunteer has told you nothing, neither the results of his counting and adding, nor the name of the card he has memorised.) Now ask him to turn over the cards one by one from the top, calling out their names as he goes. Count the cards mentally as he does this. The nineteenth card will always be the one he has memorised.
Always remember to ask the volunteer if his half pack contains between 20 and 29 cards—he needn't tell you the exact number.

EGYPT
Land of History and Mystery

by Glynn Christian

The incredible story of Egypt through the ages reads like a miniature Guinness Book of Records. The sun is hotter, the history older, the treasure more fabulous. You'll find more people packed on to a train, more water in a dam, a 57 million tonnes tomb, a queen who wore a beard and a boy-king made of gold.

Legendary river

Baked dry by the North African sun, Egypt is 96 per cent totally uninhabitable—just miles and miles of scorched desert and barren mountains. More than 30 million inhabitants have to cram themselves on to the narrow strip of fertile black soil that borders the banks of the River Nile. This makes the part of Egypt that is populated one of the most densely crowded anywhere in the world. As you might expect, even Egypt's river has special claims to fame. It's second longest in the world, yet has only two main sources, the legendary White Nile and the Blue Nile.

Four thousand miles from the Mediterranean Sea, the White Nile begins at Lake Victoria, deep in Central Africa. This fact was discovered only by the perseverance of intrepid British explorers late last century, finally solving a geographical puzzle that had perplexed man for a long time. From the lake it flows to the swamps of Southern Sudan and on to Khartoum where it meets the Blue Nile, which rises in the Highlands of Ethiopia. From that point of meeting and on through its winding path across parched Egypt to the Mediterranean, no other stream or river joins the Nile.

Unpopular April

Each year the Nile floods, depositing 110-million tonnes of rich silt along the banks. When the water recedes, the silt dries to become the famous black soil that has supported life for so long. As far as we know, people first began living on the Nile banks 6,500 years ago and even then knew enough about agriculture to raise banks and conserve the silt. The rewards for such back-breaking work were good—a remarkable climate guarantees two crops every year.

There are only two seasons here, the hot and the cold. The cold season lasts from November to April the hot from May to October. During the latter, temperatures in the south climb as high as 43°C–46°C (110°F–115°F) sometimes even more. Other than the problem of coping with such extreme heat, the most unpopular time is in April, when the **khamsin** wind blows from the desert, covering everything and everyone with a mouth-parching, yellow film of sand and dust.

Sixty-five centuries

Land workers and farmers are called **fellahin**, here. Today they live, sow, farm, plough and irrigate almost exactly the same way that Moses or Joseph of the multi-coloured coat would have seen. Precious Nile water is lifted over irrigation banks by a system of leather buckets called a **shadoof**. Blind-folded water buffaloes patiently plod around well-trodden circles, driving primitive water wheels—the **saqia**. The simple homes of the **fellahin** are still made from Nile-mud bricks, and the few, valuable farm animals owned by the family will share these living quarters during the cold season. The loin cloths of the men and robes of the women have barely changed. And their diet is still largely bread, broad beans, strong tea, goats' milk cheese and prodigious quantities of onion.

But if sixty-five centuries have not changed the **fellahin**, it's not because nothing has happened here. For this is the land of the fabled Pharaohs and their gold; of mysterious mummies and magic charms. Plus **two** of the ancient world's famous seven wonders.

Grain for Rome

Until the first pharaoh emerged in 3100 BC, Egypt was two countries, Lower Egypt and Upper Egypt. Confusingly, Lower Egypt was the more northerly, being roughly the area covered by the great delta of the Nile. South of this was Upper Egypt, mainly desert. The pharaoh paraded his mighty sovereignty of the realms by wearing a magnificent, high, double crown—a combination of the red crown of Lower Egypt and the white of Upper Egypt. Jutting menacingly from the crown's front would be a cobra's head and a vulture, both with glittering eyes of jewels and representing the countries' most powerful and vengeful gods. Although constantly conquering and being conquered, pharaohs ruled the Two Kingdoms for almost 3000 years until 33 BC. Then the scheming Cleopatra lost her country to Imperial Rome before killing herself with a snake bite. The once rich and powerful land of the pharaohs became nothing more than the granary of Rome.

The Great Pyramid

From their earliest days, the Nile dwellers believed in life after death. As the power, grandeur and wealth of the rulers and their nobles increased over the centuries, the wish for an assured life after death became stronger. It is this that enables us to know so much about these ancient people. For it led to the preserving of bodies by making them into mummies, and to the building of great tombs.

The richer you were, the stronger and more impressive you made your tomb. So it was that hundreds of thousands of slaves toiled under boiling sun to hack burial chambers from living rock or to raise pyramids, the best known of which are at Giza, on the outskirts of modern Cairo. The first pyramid was built about 4,600 years ago by a high court official called Imhotep. One hundred years later the Great Pyramid of Cheops at Giza was to dwarf it and every other building of the ancient world.

Experts can't say how long it took to build, probably thirty to forty years at least. But by translation of colourful hieroglyphics and modern scientific analysis they've worked out how it was built.

Muscle power

First a site with a solid rock base was found. Up river, huge stone blocks were cut from great granite quarries with copper chisels (this was well before the age of iron implements) then ferried down the river by a giant barge. From this point the engineers could rely only on muscle power. There were no powerful beasts of burden in ancient Egypt—no horses, no camels, not even the wheel! Surprising in a country where jealous kings of rival peoples said there was more gold than dust.

Instead huge gangs of labourers driven by the lash, sweated to heave each block off the barge, across the sand and then painfully to pile them one on top of the other—260 layers in all. You started at the bottom and strained to haul the block along a ramp that ran round all four sides of the structure, gradually sloping upwards and getting steeper and steeper. The water and buttermilk which probably cooled and lubricated the ramp meant the blocks moved more easily, but made keeping your footing more difficult.

As the pyramid grew, stonemasons chiselled out galleries, corridors and the pharaoh's burial chamber, deep in the heart. When magnificent pageantry ceremoniously laid the mummy of Pharaoh Cheops to rest, it was in a tomb covering 5 hectares. Every one of the 2,300,000 granite blocks of its construction weighed at least $2\frac{1}{2}$ tonnes, meaning the body of just one man was protected by more than 57 million tonnes of stone.

The ninety-year toothache

Egyptians believed that although the spirit left the body when someone died, it eventually came back to take its owner to another world of great joy and constant pleasure, rather like the Christian notion of Heaven. By preserving the body they hoped to make it easier for the wandering spirit to recognise its earthly body. Otherwise, body and spirit might permanently remain separated—perhaps the origin of the world-wide belief in ghosts?

It took about seventy days for the priests to prepare a mummy. A natural soda-like substance was used to dry all the moisture from the body, which was then wrapped with much ritual. Hundreds of metres of treated white linen were wound around the body, with jewellery, charms and magic talismans put between the layers according to sacred rites and instruction. The wrapped body was placed in a series of coffins, one inside the other like Russian dolls. The process of preservation worked superbly. Thirty-two centuries after he died we can still see the head of the partially unwrapped mummy of Pharaoh Rameses II, believed to be the king who drove Moses and the Hebrews from Egypt. The mummy, in Cairo Museum, has hair on the scalp and X-rays show that although healthy enough to live until he was 90, Rameses always had trouble with his gums and teeth.

Lost—a Sphinx

Close to the Pyramids of Giza is the Sphinx, completing the group of monuments that made one of the Seven Wonders of the Ancient World. Carved from a natural outcrop of rock, it is the length of a football field and seven storeys high, yet seems to have spent most of its life quite hidden. It was first excavated from the drifting sands that had shrouded it in 1500 BC. At that time the Sphinx and Pyramids were already 1000 years old and a fantastic tourist attraction. Gradually the sands crept in again until, less than a hundred years ago, travellers saw only part of the head. It was 1926 before the whole body was once more uncovered.

Boy King of Gold

Not all the pharaohs and nobles were buried in pyramids. Many tombs have been found dug into the rock and sand of the bleak Valley of Kings, across the Nile from baking Luxor. The most renowned is that of Pharaoh Tutankhamun, who ascended the throne of the Two Kingdoms when he was nine and died aged eighteen in 1352 BC.

When the explorers Howard Carter and Lord Caernarvon found his tomb in 1922, after shifting 200,000 tonnes of sand and rubble, it created a sensation throughout the entire world. Previously discovered tombs had been plundered of treasure, many even of the mummies. This one was virtually untouched, and for the first time we were able to see how a pharaoh was buried. It was truly fabulous. Jewellery, swords, statues, food, cosmetics, spare clothes, games, musical instruments, beds, tables, chairs and trinkets of unbelievable richness were packed into every corner of the tomb, all to make the king's journey to the next world more comfortable. But no one was prepared for the dazzling treasure that protected Tutankhamun's mummy. Shielded by three boxes covered in decorated gold were three coffins. Each was a breathtaking masterpiece of craftsmanship, but the inner coffin still almost defies belief. It is hand-beaten and fashioned from 132kg (296lb) of pure gold, decorated with

jewels and glistening enamel, and faithfully reproduces a portrait of the teenage king, the famous golden mask.

Yet, astonishingly, this is the tomb of a very unimportant young king. Scholars believe that all the wealth found in Tutankhamun's tomb is probably less than that once placed in just one room of the tomb of such a pharaoh as Rameses.

Dead custom

The furnishings and games found in the tomb gave us an extraordinary insight into the everyday life of the royal family and their privileged friends. Monkeys, cats and dogs were favourite pets, both the last two being taught to hunt. Even the finest houses had little furniture and few people had proper beds. For most, bed meant a pile of linen or straw on the floor—and a headrest for a pillow. Headrests, carved to fit the back of the neck were made of pottery, wood or stone. Each one had to be precision-made to fit its owner or a good night's sleep was impossible. Recent attempts to get comfortable with a headrest only led to the experimenters learning the true meaning of feeling 'dead from the neck up'! Modern visitors to Egypt will be relieved to learn the custom has long since died out.

Authentic sound

There was ample time for leisure it seems and plenty to do with that time, particularly for the young. Knucklebones were the basis for many games. There was a game like ludo and competitions to see who was best with a whipping top. Pick-a-back was played, so was leap frog and 'scissors-cut-paper'. Girls had dolls of clay and pottery and boys had balls of leather. Elaborate mechanical toys had their movements operated by pulling strings. Singing and dancing were favourite pastimes to the music of lutes, harps and flutes imported from Asia. Trumpets were also used, most often on the field of battle and in palace ceremony. A silver trumpet found close to Tutankhamun's mummy is still able to be played. Listening to a recording of it being sounded is an eerie experience—it's probably the only authentic sound from such ancient times we shall ever hear, and the high, thin notes conjure up splendid mental pictures.

Unpopular school

A civilisation capable both of stupendous building and delicate jewellery relied on high standards of education and training. Yet they used the most unwieldy system of mathematics imaginable. They were advanced enough in theory to calculate the area of a triangle and to take measurements of great accuracy, yet their actual method of multiplication and division was fantastically complicated; the system of writing down their calculations makes it seem almost impossible to use. To write the figure 999 for instance, Rameses, Cheops or any schoolchild had to write twenty-seven symbols. School must have been just as unpopular then as it can be now.

Bearded lady

Everyone who could afford it wanted a house with a garden running down to the Nile. The river was the only way to travel between many settlements, so even in 2500 BC boat building was a fine art. One enormous barge carried two stone obelisks (like Cleopatra's Needle) to the Temple of Karnak for Queen Hapshepsut. Big enough to carry the obelisks end to end, the barge was powered by thirty boats, each propelled by thirty or thirty-two strong oarsmen—at least 900 men. This was by no means the most remarkable thing done by the fascinating Hapshepsut. When she declared herself pharaoh, she donned a false beard and wore men's clothes to ensure she was regarded and obeyed as a real pharaoh and not just a woman who called herself one. Her statues and portraits show her dressed like this, much to the consternation of early historians —they couldn't work out if it was a man with a woman's name, a woman with a natural beard—or some strange god. Or was it a goddess? And if you're ready for another amazing Egyptian fact, the temple for which the obelisks of Hapshepsut were destined took over 2000 years to build.

Fingernail travellers

Today travel in Egypt is more varied. The horse and camel have arrived and modern hydrofoils or air-conditioned pleasure boats ply the Nile. Most astonishing of all are the trains. Even those who are used to the rush-hour crush of the Underground won't be prepared for the sight of an Egyptian train straining its way across the countryside. Not only will the inside of the carriages be absolutely crammed full of people, produce and animals, there'll also be families, friends and hangers-on all over the train; 'hangers-on' because that's just what they are doing, hanging on to the train by not much more

than a fingernail and a toe! But, all unconcerned, there'll be more on the roof, some more on the engine, possibly even one or two on the 'cow-catcher' in front of the engine.

Two seas joined

The modern engineering feats of Egypt are also in the record class. Perhaps the best known is the Suez Canal, finished just over one hundred years ago. The successful joining of the Mediterranean and Red Sea was first done in 2000 BC and followed a line similar to that taken by the modern canal. It had to be restored in 600 BC and 500 BC. It was once more re-opened with much ceremony in AD 642.
One hundred years later parts were filled in for military reasons and the idea was forgotten for over one thousand years.

It was during Napoleon's occupation of Egypt in 1798–1801 that the idea was seriously considered again. Bungling officialdom took another fifty years to get work started. Then the massive use of manpower that had raised pyramids was once again seen in Egypt. At first 25,000 men were employed, but after giant mechanical dredges were introduced, the labour force was reduced to 10–18,000 men. When the Suez Canal was opened in 1869, 97 million cubic metres of earth had been excavated. Of the 101 miles from Port Said on the Mediterranean to Suez on the Red Sea, ninety-two miles have been hacked from the land; the other nine miles were natural waterways.

In the early days it took ships forty-eight hours to complete the canal journey, now it's only fifteen hours. Use of the canal saves long-haul ships anything up to 70 per cent of their fuel bills, to say nothing of time.

Jig-saw monuments

The far south of Upper Egypt now proudly features a feat of gargantuan proportions. This is the Aswan Dam, built to control the flooding waters of the Nile, provide cheap electricity and to irrigate just under half a million hectares of otherwise useless land.

The dam's base is over 800m (½-mile) thick and over 105m (350ft) high. Its length is almost 4km (2½ miles) and holds back a mass of water 545km (340 miles) long and 9km (5½ miles) wide. Much of the area flooded contained priceless relics of the country's heritage. So thousands of tons of ancient carved statues, temples and monuments were carefully sawn into manageable pieces and reassembled high above the new water level.

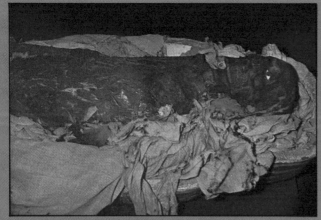
The blackened flesh of a mummy after preservation.

Colossal statues of Rameses II at Abu Simbel.

The Alabaster mosque in Central Cairo.

The head of Nefertiti, an Egyptian queen of 3,000 years ago.

Covered bazaars

Bustling Cairo, biggest city in Africa and the Middle East, resounds to romantic tales of Saladin, the Crusades and a glorious past: Alexandria, on the Mediterranean, was the site of another of the Seven Wonders, the world's greatest lighthouse. In both cities and in many towns and villages the most exciting thing the visitor can do is to visit the covered bazaar, immersing himself in the din, colour and customs of another age. In tiny, shadowy booths and stalls, the smells of freshly-ground herbs and spices mix with the sharp tang of leather being worked by children. Exotic perfumes made from orange blossoms, rose petals, lotus flowers, jasmine and sandalwood are sold close to workshops where tiny fingers embroider robes, tap patterns into

Jenny and Mick travelling Egyptian-style!

The fertile black soil bordering the banks of the Nile.

A wall carving of huntsmen spearing their prey.

An alabaster sphinx at Memphis, remarkably well preserved.

brass trays or knead dough for flat bread. This, too, is part of Egypt that has changed little.

After a morning spent in furious bargaining for the goods you want, you might find yourself sitting at a café terrace sipping hot mint tea, while the wail of exotic music wafts from a tiny alley. Close your eyes and you could be back in the time of the pharaohs. The papyrus they used no longer grows in Egypt. But the bazaars are still there. The **fellahin** are. The Nile is. And somewhere under the hot, dusty, shifting desert sands lies a tomb of pharaoh's treasure that will be unplundered and unseen by man for over three thousand years. Perhaps you are the High Priest who sealed the door to that tomb. You might even be the new pharaoh. . . .

On Safari

by Tony Gray

In a safari camp the day begins early—as early as 4.30 am. If you are watching wild animals, the first thing you must do is to go on to the animals' schedule. And some of the predators—lions and leopards, for example—hunt at night and sleep all day. Lions sleep most of the time—up to twenty hours a day.

The best time to see them is as soon as possible after first light. So it's a quick cup of tea and then pile into the jeep or land rover; most of them have bars rigged along the side as a protection. It's always a bumpy ride through the bush. Many of the private game reserves in South Africa, like the one which I visited, have no roads and no bridges. You drive straight through the rivers, down one bank, across the riverbed, and up the other. Mind you, most of the time this is no problem because the rivers are as dry as the Sahara desert for three hundred days every year. And when the rains come, they're raging torrents, three to four metres deep, and nobody goes anywhere.

Once outside the camp stockade, you are in the middle of the wildlife. Screaming francolin—a wild pheasant with a bright red head—dart from under the wheels. From above the treetops giraffe stare curiously at the jeep before casually loping away. Herds of impala fly across the track in front of the vehicle; some of them leap 2m (6ft) into the air. Kudu, another variety of antelope, with moist intelligent eyes and huge quivering ears, stand and watch the metal monster guardedly. White rhino—curiously called, because they are really a reddish black—lumber around ponderously. With their lethal horns and terrifying bulk, they're very frightening, and yet they're completely timid: they're only dangerous because they are almost totally blind and could easily crush the jeep to pulp by mistake if anything upset them. A herd of elephants appear—these are the most dangerous of all the animals: even lions are uneasy when there are elephants around. Of all the wild animals, only elephants and lions have no natural enemies apart from man; there is no creature that will try to kill any of them. They are eaten only as carrion, or dead flesh, when they have died naturally.

The game wardens and safari drivers always steer well clear of elephants; if there are calves in the herd, they will charge anything that moves, and they could demolish a jeep without even suffering a headache. Sometimes they uproot trees, because they like to eat the roots as well as the leaves and the bark. Vast areas of the South African bush are littered with dead trees pushed over and smashed by elephants.

Vultures circling in the sky and perched in trees indicate a recent kill in the vicinity; they are waiting until the predators have satisfied their hunger, when they hope to dart in to grab some food. When they see vultures, the drivers of the jeeps and land rovers slow down and start to hunt around. If you're lucky, you may come across a pride of lions, feeding on an animal which they've killed during the hours of darkness. A pride of lions usually consists of one or two adult males, up to half a dozen lionesses, and a selection of cubs of various ages. The lionesses do almost all the hunting—they're leaner and faster than the males and don't have the encumbrance of a mane—and the meal is served in very strict order: first the pride males, then the lionesses, in order of seniority, and then the cubs, the smallest and weakest last. The male lions mark and guard the range, the territory of the pride; that is their contribution.

Most of the prey (animals on which the lions feed), such as impala, wildebeest, warthog and giraffe, can run much faster than they can, so the lions must rely on camouflage and surprise; unless they get to their prey before it gets into the right gear, they cannot possibly catch it. Because of this the lions don't necessarily make a kill every night and, consequently, when they do make a kill, they gorge themselves. By filling themselves like this, lions can last for about a week between kills.

A herd of zebra at the water hole.

When you have found the lions on a kill, you watch them and photograph them for a couple of hours. Then you can go away, knowing that they will still be there in exactly the same spot, that evening. When they have finished eating, they usually rest under a shingayi tree—a form of acacia, which is umbrella-shaped, which offers enough shade for a whole pride.

You then drive back to the camp for brunch: fresh paw-paws or mangoes, a sort of porridge made from the local mealie-meal which is a bit like semolina; sausages made from impala; and coffee with powdered milk. There's no milkman and no postman in the bush. The nearest town is over fifty miles away and you have to drive there to collect your mail.

The whole existence there is very close to nature. After dark, you must carry a torch at all times; otherwise, you might disturb a snake or a scorpion. The very food you eat is the wildlife you have been watching: impala, francolin, guinea fowl, warthog. And the game warden and safari drivers spend a proportion of the time 'shooting for the pot'—in other words, killing game for the rations.

In high summer—which in the Transvaal comes at Christmas time—it is too hot to do anything except lie down between twelve and three. Then, after a cool shower (the water is never cold), you might go out in the jeep again, around four o'clock.

A pair of lions asleep—their favourite daytime occupation!

A herd of buffalo pounding through the bush.

A white rhino is really reddish black in colour.

No two drives through the bush are ever the same. This time you might be threatened by a spitting cobra which suddenly rears up in the track ahead of you, hood extended and spitting at the car. You can be thankful for the windscreen because a spitting cobra can kill a man at 10 metres, spitting into his eyes with deadly accuracy. All of the camps and most of the jeeps are equipped with serum kits: they have to be, because there are snakes around like the black mamba and if you are bitten by one of these, you have exactly ten minutes to live.

Eventually you reach the place where you left the lions. They are still there, dozing in the last weak rays of the sun. Now they begin to stir. One lioness will get up, walk a few paces, and flop down again. Another will rouse herself, attempt to awaken a couple of the cubs, and then subside on the sand for another doze. The whole business is a bit like watching an orchestra warming up. Finally one of them—usually the dominant lioness—will succeed in getting the show on the road. Reluctantly—and the pride males are always the last to give in—they will all stagger to their feet, shake the sleep from their eyes, and head into the bush for another night's hunting.

You drive back to the camp through a magical twilight, the headlamps of the jeep picking up the reflections of countless pairs of eyes—impala or lion, it's impossible to say. Behind the jeep, like the phosphorescent wake of a dinghy, there are dancing points of bright, bright light—the fireflies. Families of baboon and vervet monkeys make their way across the track and suddenly a leopard growls; it's a noise like a saw and raises the hair on the back of your neck. Of all the animals in the bush, the leopard is the hardest to see. It hunts at dead of night in the thick bush and then takes its kill into a tree where it holes up all day, invisible because of its spotted camouflage among the leafy shadows.

Back at the camp, there's impala stew for dinner, a rich savoury mixture, with sweet potatoes and avocado and a wonderful local melon. You feel a bit uneasy perhaps about the impala and zebra skins on the floor —you are remembering how beautiful and full of life they looked, running through the trees—and then you remember that the game warden told you that if their numbers were not kept strictly in check, they'd eat themselves out of house and home and would all die the next time there was a drought. And you suddenly realise, how close life and death are together, here in the wilderness.

An elephant and baby crossing a road outside one of the Safari camps.

The Houses of Parliament

The Houses of Parliament are contained within a royal palace—the Palace of Westminster. Parliament consists of three branches: the Sovereign, the Lords and the Commons, all of which have a role to play in law-making, even though, in the case of the Queen, this is purely nominal.

Victoria Tower, where the records of the Houses of Parliament are kept. It is one of the highest masonry towers in Europe, and is 98m (323ft) high and 23m (75ft) square. When Parliament is in session, a large Union Jack flies from its flagstaff.

The Terrace of the Palace of Westminster is one of the greatest amenities of the place. It stretches 206m (678ft) along the river Thames, and affords a pleasant place for Lords and MPs to relax, eat and drink during the long summer sittings.

The Lord High Chancellor's residence. He is the equivalent to the Speaker in the House of Lords, and is the highest law officer of the country.

The House of Lords Library —a 'gentleman's library' of great calm and learning.

Information supplied by Matthew Cooper

The House of Lords' half of the Palace.

The House of Commons' half of the Palace.

The Clock Tower is 96m (316 ft) high and you must climb 334 steps to reach the belfry.

The spire which stands over the Central Lobby, where Members of Parliament meet their constituents who come to 'lobby', or talk, with them.

Big Ben is not a clock, it is the name of the bell, cast in Whitechapel Bell Foundry in 1858, which is now housed in the Clock Tower. Each of the clock's four faces is 7m (23ft) in diameter and contains over 300 pieces of glass. Big Ben itself is 2.7m (9ft) in diameter and 2.3m (7½ft) high—it weighs over 13,700 kg. (13 tons).

The Banqueting Rooms, which look on to the Terrace, where MPs can entertain large groups to lunch or dinner. Wedding receptions can also be held here.

Members' Dining Rooms, one of which is for MPs alone, the other for them and their guests.

The House of Commons Library, which provides excellent research facilities for MPs.

The Upper Committee floor, where there are Members' offices and television rooms.

The Stranger's Bar, where MPs can take guests for a drink at any time while the House is sitting.

The Lords Bar, where secretaries and staff of both Houses can buy drinks.

Committee Rooms, where amendments to Bills are debated in detail, where certain aspects of society are scrutinised, and where party meetings are held.

The Speaker's Residence, a fine suite of rooms where the Speaker lives and entertains visiting dignitaries.

Working Horses and Ponies

by Toni Webber

A team of sturdy little Shetland ponies pulling a carriage.

Surprisingly, the best place to see horses at work is where it has always been—in the big cities. Even today, city streets know the clip-clop of hoofs and the rattle of wagon wheels as horses, fulfilling their ancient role as servants to man, pass their working days in the company of double-decker buses, big lorries, cars and delivery vans.

A century ago, all traffic in town or country was horse-drawn. Now, a horse-drawn vehicle is a rare sight in the country and people will stop what they are doing to watch one go by. But town shoppers will pass a brewer's dray or totter's cart without a second glance.

Brewery horses are the most spectacular of the everyday working animals. Usually they work in pairs, hauling heavy carts loaded with barrels of beer and crates of bottles for delivery to public houses. While the barrels are removed, they stand quietly in the busy street, indifferent to petrol fumes and honking horns, peacefully munching a feed from their nosebags. Sometimes, they are Shire horses, taller than a man, believed to be descended from the medieval war horses of

England. They have strong, massive bodies and great shaggy legs, but they are so docile they are often called gentle giants. Other brewery horses may be Clydesdales, a Scottish breed which is very similar to the Shire, or Suffolk Punches, which are always chestnut in colour and have very little 'feather' on their legs. Another popular heavy breed is the Percheron, a showy horse originally from France, which, like the Suffolk Punch, is clean-legged. Brewery horses are a source of great pride to the men who care for them, groom them until they shine and polish the harness until the leatherwork is supple and the brass gleams.

Totter's ponies are more familiar in suburban streets than in the heart of the city. They are rarely as showy as the brewery horses and are usually of no special breed. Their loads of old rags or scrap metal are unromantic but they have a cheeky lift to their heads which is endearing. People may wonder why their owners do not switch to motor-driven vans and trucks, but the pony is regarded by the totter with as much affection as his own family. In any case, no van could find its

Cicero the drum horse.

The coronation coach on its way through the Mall.

The Blues and Royals trooping the colour.

A mounted policeman in London.

way home at the end of the day without help from its tired driver. The totter's pony can, for most horses have an excellent homing instinct.

Although both brewery horses and totter's ponies could be replaced by motor vehicles, there is one type of city horse which could never find a substitute. This is the **police horse**, which plays such an important part in controlling crowds and performing special duties on ceremonial occasions. London has the largest number of working police horses, but there are several attached to the police forces of many other British cities.

If you have watched the ceremony of Trooping the Colour at the Queen's Birthday Parade either on television or as part of the crowd of spectators, you may have been impressed with the behaviour of the horses on parade. The Queen herself rides a police horse, but the troopers are mounted on Army horses. These **cavalry horses** are no longer used in warfare but trained for ceremonies and parades, sporting activities such as show-jumping and eventing, and public entertainments like tattoos, musical rides and tent-pegging contests.

Whenever there are likely to be large crowds present, ceremonial horses have to be carefully trained. The **carriage horses** in the Royal Mews at Buckingham Palace, for example, have to learn to cope with the sound of cheering and loud music, shrill whistles and waving flags.

The most famous of the Royal carriage horses is the team of greys. They draw the Irish State Coach when the Queen travels to Westminster for the annual State Opening of Parliament; their predecessors pulled the Gold State Coach at the Coronation. The Coronation was a particularly arduous ritual for the horses: during the ceremony, whilst the Queen was being crowned in Westminster Abbey, the eight horses had to wait in the cold and rain in all their trappings, missing their mid-day feed because it was not possible to give them anything to eat. All behaved impeccably.

Many horses, it seems, enjoy crowds and like showing off before an admiring audience. The horses you see in circuses often work better during an actual performance than at rehearsals. The teams of plumed horses, which seem to 'dance'

A fine pair of horses in a ploughing competition.

A horse-drawn milk float on show at Windsor.

to the music, pirouette and make diagonal movements across the ring, are known as **Liberty horses.** Many of them are Arab or part-Arab and their polished performance is the result of three or four years' training in high school work, an equestrian art which dates back hundreds of years.

The horse on which the bareback rider performs her tricks is called a **resinback**: his breed is immaterial for he is always chosen for his broad back, placid temperament and easy paces. Nothing worries him—his rider can swing from his mane and clowns cling to his tail, but he takes it all in good part. Shetland ponies and their even smaller cousins from Argentina, Falabella ponies, make excellent circus acts. They are so round, woolly and appealing, with a mischievous gleam in their eye, that audiences adore them.

Shetlands, of course, in spite of their size, have been working ponies for centuries. Although, nowadays, they are mostly bred as riding ponies for children, in their native Shetland isles, they are still used as **pack ponies**, carrying bulky loads over rough ground without tiring or losing their footing.

Perhaps the best-loved working horse of all, but seldom seen nowadays, is the **farm horse**. Like brewery horses, he is usually one of the heavy breeds—the gentle Shire, the powerful Clydesdale or the lively Suffolk Punch. Some farms kept a large number of horses, generally used singly or in pairs, occasionally in teams of three, four or six. They had names like Boxer or Blossom and their

great strength pulled ploughs, harrows or hay wagons as easily as a child pulls a wheeled toy. Fortunately, for the sake of these noble horses, there are still a few farmers who like to keep a heavy horse around the place, finding him more useful than a tractor for some of the jobs on the farm. In fact, during a recent exceptionally wet spring, when even tractors were getting bogged down in the mud, farmers with horses were able to get ahead with their spring sowing, for the animals' big feet did less damage to the rain-sodden ground than the wheels of the tractor. Interest in heavy horses is reviving, and ploughing contests, once a regular feature of country life, are now more widely held and always attract a big attendance.

The main virtues of all working horses are strength, stamina and a willingness to learn. Some, however, have yet another quality—the ability to inspire confidence in other creatures. The **herding ponies**, for instance, used by shepherds in the hilly country of Wales and Cumbria can calm a panicking sheep more quickly than the human voice. A stray sheep, lifted bleating and struggling across the saddle of the shepherd's pony, will rest quietly in this uncomfortable position throughout the long trek homewards.

Perhaps this is why working horses—as opposed to those used purely for recreation or sport—will never completely disappear. There are some qualities which no machine could ever duplicate.

The Night Has a Thousand Eyes

by John Huins

The sun has fallen below the horizon, and the first stars are showing. As the darkness of night arrives, the living world prepares to sleep. Yet even as our day is ending, another world is awakening. It's a strange and enchanted world which few humans ever know, with its own species, its own sounds, and its own rules for survival.

Creatures of the Dark

For early man, night was a time of hostility and fear. Even today, superstitions abound of 'ghoulies and ghosties and long-leggety beasties and things that go bump in the night'. We are safe in our artificially lit and heated homes, which re-create the daytime environment. We can scarcely imagine the terrors that could strike if we found ourselves lost on Dartmoor on a moonless night. We even avoid the dimly lit alleyways of the town. Yet these places where humans fear to tread are the natural habitat for thousands of creatures.

In fact few animals are totally nocturnal. Dawn and dusk are the periods of most activity, as you'll know if you have ever taken a late evening or early morning walk in the woods. Even with the specially-attuned eyesight most nocturnals share, a certain amount of light is necessary to see. Nevertheless, it is the night that gives all these animals a common world, that can be alien and dangerous to daytime creatures like man.

The domestic cat, for example, which seems docile and dozy during the day, is transformed when it goes out on its midnight prowl. The cat is equipped for night life: it can see in the dark, its fur often provides camouflage, and its instincts of both hunting and self-preservation are sharpened by the night. And for the countless stray cats, and the wild cats that live in Scotland, the night brings both security and food.

Rodents are one of the biggest groups of nocturnal creatures. Rats, voles and mice thrive in both city and country. At dusk they emerge to forage for food, and they have big appetites, often eating a third of their own weight each night. In the city there is no lack of food and rodents benefit from the natural disguise of their dull brown or grey coats. Yet the minute they move they are in danger from the sharp, preying eyes of their enemies.

Their enemies are many. In the country they include weasels and stoats that have an agility and savagery to

The fox, one of the most feared night hunters.

The long-eared owl a daunting bird of prey.

render most rodents defenceless. There are other predators on rodents who are equally at home in the country and in the city—owls, bats, and even foxes.

The reason wild creatures settle in town is simple—food and shelter. Few people realise how many mice and rats inhabit our cities, and yet the rodent population of most places actually outnumbers the human population. We are unaware of them because they are night creatures. Dustbins, compost heaps and refuse tips are an almost inexhaustible source of food. And any creature that eats in these places is himself potential food for another.

With their acute sense of smell and their vivid cat-like eyes, foxes have always been one of the countryside's most feared night-hunters. Now, increasingly, they are moving into the city outskirts, living in parks and allotments, and hunting the streets at night. This new generation of town foxes has abandoned the rabbits and hens of the country for the rats, mice and dustbin scraps of the town.

As the fox depends on its sense of smell, so the owl, one of the few nocturnal birds, relies strongly on its hearing, and its fast and silent flight. The common tawny owl, which can kill creatures twice its own size, generally lives in woods and forests, but the barn owl will nest happily in rooftops and deserted buildings. The barn owl is an excellent example of how a creature's anatomy is suited to night hunting. Having first seen the prey, it then hunts almost exclusively by sound; its large ears receive sound waves trapped by and reflected from the flat facial disc, a finely-tuned technique not unlike the vast radio receivers of Jodrell Bank.

Even more remarkable is the way bats use sound to locate their prey. Contrary to common belief bats are not blind, nevertheless their main navigational tool is not eyesight, but sound echoes. They fly in swarms, in and out of caves, church belfries, or rooftops, without hitting each other, and at the same time tracking and eating flying insects that are their main diet. They do it by means of a technique similar to the wartime ASDIC system. That is, they send out a series of high-pitched squeaks beyond the human range of hearing. These squeaking calls are emitted at a rate of between ten and sixty a second, and the time it takes for the echoes to return enables the bat to locate the prey or obstacle. Bats are agile flyers, and catch their prey either in their mouths, or in the wing membranes.

These are just some of the multitude of species that thrive at night. As we've seen, the night is rarely as tranquil as it seems. Indeed, night living is largely a question of hunting and being hunted, and 'survival of the fittest' is the only rule. The cat is the one creature

A tree shrew.

A hairy armadillo.

A vampire bat.

An edible dormouse.

A group of spiny mice.

A Siberian chipmunk.

we have discussed that usually has an independent food supply, and even the cat spends the night following its basic hunting instinct.

Virtually all night life relies on disguise, concealment, sharp senses and fast reflexes for two simple ends—self-preservation and finding food. It is no surprise that man is a stranger in this world, for in all these respects man is an inferior species to these natural inhabitants of the night.

Different species of all these creatures of the night—cats, rodents, foxes, owls, bats, insects—are to be found on every continent of the world. All are common in most parts of Britain, too. The variety is immense within each species. There are, for example, 2,000 known species of rodent in the world, and at least 1,000 different bats. In the living desert, at night—amid the seemingly lifeless wastes—there are dancing scorpions, wriggling millipedes, bulbous toads hunting beetles at the waterholes; there are bats that hang from cave roofs in the daytime, and at night swarm in their millions consuming insects by the ton; there are snakes and lizards, and rats that jump up and down; there are wild desert cats with big round dark eyes, and there are owls; one species hardly ever found in the desert night is man.

The delightful bushbaby, a native of Africa, inhabits the forest where he prowls the trees at night in search of crickets, grasshoppers, praying mantis, fruit and birds' eggs. The bushbaby can leap two metres with no difficulty, and will do so at the slightest sign of danger (which its large ears are quick to note). It has large eyes for one simple reason: to take in as much light as possible.

These big, bulbous eyes are common to a wide range of creatures, some related to the bushbaby, and others which have evolved independently to reach a similar appearance. They are all very attractive and prove major attractions at any zoo—from the tailless slender loris from India, which sleeps all day rolled into a fur ball, to the charming aye-aye from Malagasy, with its thick silvery fur and the thin fingers it uses to extract larvae from trees or sugar from the cane. Tarsiers and opossums are two more favourite large-eyed animals that lead a similar night life.

The tiny vampire bat, which inhabits caves and hollow trees throughout South America, lives solely on blood and must suck 28 grams every night to live. After a day's sleep, hanging upside down, the vampires emerge at dusk and swoop across trees and rivers in search of large mammals and sleeping birds. They home in on their prey like guided missiles. Their sharp-edged incisors scoop out a piece of skin (usually painlessly) and the bat laps the blood of its sleeping victim.

As angwantibo, its eyes reflecting a bright light.

It is virtually impossible to go 'into the wild' and observe the moonlight world in action. Even if you could see in the dark, any creature of the night would have sensed your presence, and fled or hidden as you approached. Nevertheless, it is not difficult to construct an artificial environment that re-creates the conditions and light cycle of the night. If a nocturnal species is introduced into the correctly-constructed environment, it can live, thrive and even reproduce, unaware that its world is man-made, or that man is observing its everyday life.

This has been done to dramatic effect in several zoos of the world. Artificial 'Moonlight Worlds' have been constructed and visitors walk through a darkened gallery to see assorted nocturnal creatures in their natural habitats. At London Zoo, for example, over 200 nocturnal animals can be observed. At night, the cage lighting brightens, so the creatures follow their daytime behaviour and rest. Thus when the zoo is open the cage lighting dims, the illusion of night sends the nocturnal inhabitants on their active and awake behaviour pattern. This is taken a step further by reversing the seasons as well, so that what is for us the longest daylight period becomes for the Moonlight World inhabitants their longest night. In simple terms, this means that London's Moonlight World is based on Australian time—six months, and twelve hours out of phase.

London Zoo has an excellent record with its nocturnal life, due to the immense care taken for the animals' welfare. Temperature, humidity and even the diet's protein content are monitored and controlled. The animals adapt happily to this life. Several species reproduce regularly in captivity, including the rare fennec fox. Bushbabies, lorises, vampire and fruit bats, civets, genets and leopard cats have all produced offspring. Not long ago, four Russian dwarf hamsters were introduced into one of the fifty cages. Within nine months, those four had reproduced no fewer than two hundred offspring!

Make your own Moonlight World

If you already have a pet animal which, if in the wild would, prefer the night—a mouse, hamster or gerbil for example—you may have thought it is rather shy, or sleepy. This is no surprise, since daytime is its natural sleeping time.

However, it is easy to re-create the night-time habitat in your own home using the simple method employed by London Zoo to make its Moonlight World. The basic idea is to turn night into day and day into night, by artificially lighting the habitat at night and shutting out the daylight. Thus, during the day your animals will be in the dark and at their most active, while during our night, when the cage lights come on, the animals go into their dens to sleep.

You will need:

Pet(s) and cage. Make certain your pet is nocturnal. A dark room. An under-stairs cupboard or spare room (with curtains that can be drawn) would be ideal, although ensure there is sufficient ventilation and enough heating in winter.
A 40-watt light-bulb and a 15-watt night light.

To create the night light cycle:

Ask your parents to extend the flex on the ceiling light fitting so as to fix the bulb as close to the cage front as possible, while ensuring it cannot get near to any bedding and is not within the reach of your pet. Use a 40-watt bulb. This light should be switched on every evening and switched off in the morning, with a 12 hours on and 12 hours off cycle. This process can be made automatic by asking your parents to fit a standard time-switch. When you want to look at your pets you will have to use a weak bulb giving you enough light to see your pets, while maintaining the illusion of night for them. A 15-watt night light concealed behind the cage, or shaded to reduce light directed at the animals, will be ample.

To watch your Moonlight World:

In the daytime, the room containing your Moonlight World should be kept dark with only the night light on. To view the animals, enter as quietly as possible. Having allowed time for your eyes to adjust to darkness, you should then be able to observe them in a fully active and uninhibited state. Maintenance such as food, water and cleaning should be continued as usual for your pet.

With grateful thanks to Dr Brambell, Curator of Mammals and Guardian of the Moonlight World at London Zoo, for his advice in preparing this article.

Crack the Code

ZNK SGMVOK HKRUTMY ZU ZNK IXUC LGSORE. ZNK
IUSSUT SGMVOK NGY HRGIQ GTJ CNOZK VRASGMK
GTJ G RUTM ZGOR. OZ LKKJY UT OTYKIZY, YTGORY
GTJ SOIK GTJ ULZKT XUHY UZNKX HOXJY TKYZY UL
KMMY GTJ EUATM. OZ NOJKY YAXVRGY LUUJ GTJ
GRYU GTE IUXUAXLGX UX YNOTE UHPKIZY CNOIN
GZZXGIZ OZY GZZKTZOUT. OZ OY LUATJ OT KAXUVK,
GYOG GTJ TUXZN GLXOIG (see page 128 for the answer)

LAUGH IF YOU LIKE — BUT I HEARD SOMETHING DOWN THERE!

GIVE ME A HAND TO CARRY MY POCKET
MONEY — DAD OWES ME TWO WEEKS!

Get it All Mapped Out!

by Deborah Manley and Pamela Cotterill

To be a good map reader, it's no use just poring over exciting maps at home, although this will give you invaluable help in 'picking-up' the knack of reading them. *Use* them whenever you can, in streets, at the seaside, in the hills, and then study them at home so that you can conjure up remembered pictures of what you've seen and relate to the symbols on the map. If you are to visit relatives or friends in another town, get an Ordnance Survey map of the area on the scale 1:50,000 so you can get the town in its landscape perspective and see its relationship to other towns and villages and rivers and canals and railways. Then get a larger scale map or plan of the town and use it to explore the streets and interesting byways. When I was in the North recently, I used a street plan to explore stretches of the river and canal and some derelict wasteland, and was able to form a vivid impression of how my home town has developed and decayed since the Industrial Revolution.

If you are going out in a car, offer to be the 'back-seat' driver, that is the navigator using the map to guide the driver. With a good road map you can find interesting ways off the main roads when the route is boring, or when you are snarled up in bank holiday traffic jams. Many country roads are deserted now that a network of motorways covers the country, and although they may add miles to your journey they may save time in the end. They are often narrow and they wind more than motorways, but country roads pass through pretty villages and lovely countryside that you would miss on the motorway. When driving through a town a street plan will enable you to avoid traffic jams which may occur during the 'rush hour' when people are leaving work.

Understanding the scale of the map

One of the first things you need to know when you look at a map is: How large is the area it covers? How far is it from one place to another? On a map the real distance on the ground is shown by a much smaller distance on paper. 100 metres on the ground might be shown by only 1cm on a map. We call this relationship the scale of the map. It should always be given on the map. There are three ways in which it can be shown:

1 In words:

Scale 1cm = 1 metre
or one centimetre represents 30 kilometres

2 With a plain scale:

Kilometres

The distance between each point on this plain scale represents one kilometre on the ground.

3 Using Representative Fraction (RF):

This is a bit more complex, but read carefully and you'll understand. Let's say that the scale on the map is: 1cm = 1km. Now, how many centimetres are there in a kilometre? 100,000. So you can show this scale as a fraction, like this: $\frac{1}{100,000}$ or like this: 1:100,000.

The great advantage of RF is that it is equally true whatever unit of measure you are using. For example, if you are using feet and inches, then one inch on the map will represent 100,000 inches on the ground. Now, try for yourself.

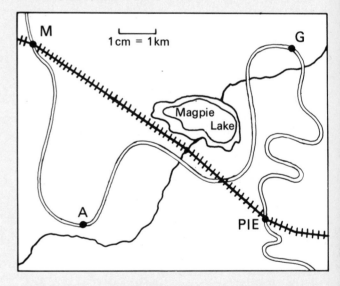

1cm = 1km

How far is it from Masterton (M) to Appleborough (A) to Gantry (G) to Pie Hill (Pie) as the crow flies? But you can't always go as the crow flies can you? On this map the roads wind and you might well have to follow them. How far would it be from Appleborough to Gantry by road? Take a piece of string. Lay it along the road and mark the positions of Appleborough and Gantry on it with a ballpoint pen. Measure the distance between those two marks with your ruler. You should find that it is 10km from Appleborough to Gantry.

Looking for Landmarks

Maps can show us a lot of things. They show us how far apart places are and how high and low the land is and how steeply you will have to climb in hilly country. They can also show us what we will see on the way. They show us landmarks by using symbols. Sometimes these are little pictures; sometimes they are initial letters and sometimes they are different sorts of lines. You can see a selection of symbols and lines illustrated below. Try and memorise them.

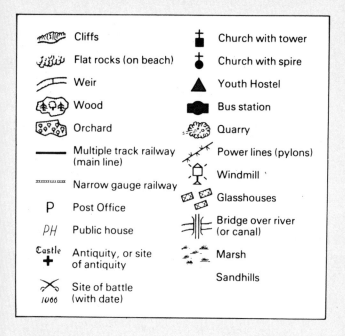

Cliffs	Church with tower
Flat rocks (on beach)	Church with spire
Weir	Youth Hostel
Wood	Bus station
Orchard	Quarry
Multiple track railway (main line)	Power lines (pylons)
Narrow gauge railway	Windmill
P Post Office	Glasshouses
PH Public house	Bridge over river (or canal)
Castle Antiquity, or site of antiquity	Marsh
1066 Site of battle (with date)	Sandhills

Which Way?

Everyone knows there are four main or cardinal points of direction: north (N), south (S), east (E), and west (W). North is the direction of the North Pole. A good way to find North at night is by locating the group of stars known as the Plough; the two 'pointers' point directly at the Pole Star which is overhead at the North Pole and thus gives the direction for the North. Face the Pole Star; behind you is S, on your right is E and on your left W.

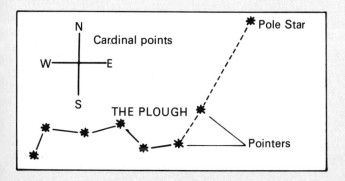

The sun is another good way of finding the approximate direction, for it rises in the east and sets in the west. At midday during winter time (Greenwich Mean Time) the sun is due south.

Between the main direction points are four intermediate points: north-east (NE), south-east (SE), south-west (SW) and north-west (NW). There are further subdivisions too. Between N and NE is north-north-east (NNE) and between NE and E is ENE. See if you can name the other subdivisions, and write them in on the diagram. (See Answers, page 128)

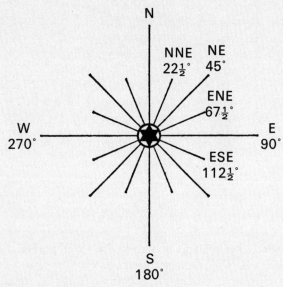

Using a compass

Direction can be measured just as height can. We measure direction with a compass, and it is a good idea for you to know something about the compass, for if your map reading excursions take you off the beaten track and into hills and moorlands, it will be essential for you to have, in addition to your map, a compass and the knowledge how to use it. The compass works on the principle that a magnetised strip of metal, freely suspended, always points to *magnetic* north, which is just a few degrees off true north at the North Pole. A circle has 360 degrees (imagine a huge cake cut into 360 equal slices) and so counting N as zero, by turning the compass housing round, the angle between the north-pointing needle and the direction of travel can be measured in degrees. East is 90, south is 180, west is 270. If you are mathematically inclined you can work out the bearings for NE, SE, SW and NW and write them in on the diagram above. The compass is most useful in mist when travelling across country, for when you can't see very far ahead, the compass bearing gives you the true direction to follow. See if you can find the wild crested dragon in the game overleaf.

Find the wild crested dragon

Here is a game using the points of the compass.

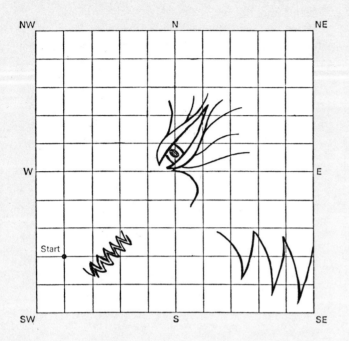

9	100	SE
10	100	NE
11	100	S
12	100	NE
13	100	S
14	100	E
15	100	SW
16	100	E
17	100	SW
18	100	E
19	100	SW
20	100	E
21	100	SW
22	100	NW
23	300	S
24	300	W
25	300	SW
26	100	N
27	150	NW
28	50	NE
29	150	SW
30	50	NW

There is a fabulous dragon hidden in these squares. He regularly eats the citizens of Nanthyranthypoo in the land of Lilipalala. No one has ever seen him except for the people he has eaten—and they had only a passing acquaintance! But, according to legend, once his likeness has been portrayed his power will die and he will wither and perish.

How to play

Each side of each square represents 100 metres. Now, with a pen or pencil, follow the directions, drawing a line from the point *start*. But hurry! The people of Nanthyranthypoo are relying on you to break the dragon's power!

(All figures are given in metres. If you can't find the dragon, turn to the Answers on page 128.)

Directions:

1 move	300 metres	NE
2	100	NW
3	200	NE
4	100	NW
5	100	E
6	100	N
7	100	SE
8	100	N

Other ways of finding direction

The stump of a felled tree can give you a clue, for the bark and growth rings are thicker on the north side where less sunlight has fallen on the tree during its growth. Trees are often shaped by the prevailing winds. The tree leans in the direction of the wind and short branches face the wind. In the British Isles the damp south-westerly winds are the most common prevailing winds so isolated trees tend to lean NE. The altar is usually at the east end of a church. Moss grows better on the sheltered east or north-eastern sides of trees. You can use your watch to find direction too. Hold your watch horizontally so that the hour hand points into the sun. Ignore the minute hand completely. Now trace an imaginary line between the hour hand and the twelve on the watch face—this gives you approximate direction of south. During British Summer Time (March–October), or Central European Time, take the line between the figure 1 and the hour hand to find the south.

Reading the shape of the land

Showing the relief, that is the shape of the land, is quite a problem for mapmakers, for how do you show three-dimensional shapes on a flat map? The answer to this problem lay in the use of contour lines.

A contour line is a drawn line, linking all places at the same height. Contour lines indicate vertical height and they also tell us something about the degree of slope, whether it is steep or gradual. Draw some contour lines for yourself to see how they work. Get a large ball and some chalk. As the ball is round, your contours will be round too. Decide on a suitable interval for the contour lines; on a large ball perhaps 4cm, 1cm for a tennis ball. Use a vertically placed ruler to mark the intervals on the ball, as shown below.

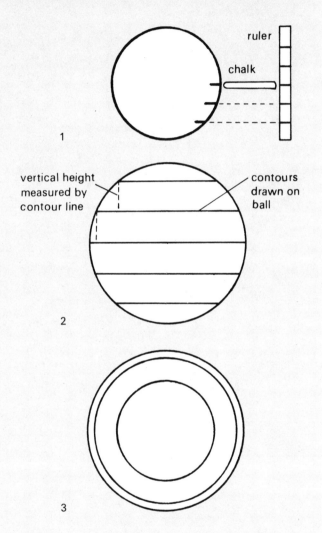

When you have drawn the contours around the ball it will look like drawing 2 above. Look at it from on top and it will look like drawing 3. This shows you a lot about contour lines. On a map, contour lines like this would represent a perfectly rounded hill (of course you can't see the 'contours' on the bottom of the ball). The contour lines that are close together show steep slopes (round the middle of the ball); where they are more spaced out the slopes are gentler.

This article is taken from *Maps and Map Games* published by Piccolo.

How to become a professional mapmaker

If you become really interested in maps and mapmaking, you may like to know about two careers where you could work and use your interest. One is that of a cartographer; the other that of a surveyor of land or of water.

The surveyor does the measuring of roads, buildings, hills, valleys and other features, and records them in their correct positions so that the cartographer can revise maps such as the Ordnance Survey map, and keep them up to date.

Most cartographers work for the government but they may also be employed (usually on a freelance arrangement—that is, working at home and being paid for the work done) by publishers and by tourist organisations to make maps for books, travel pamphlets and guides. Think of all the travel books, the atlases, the school textbooks and tourist guides which have maps. Many of these maps, particularly the more detailed ones, are drawn by cartographers.

To train as a cartographer you will need passes in the General Certificate of Education (GCE) Ordinary ('O') Level or Grade One Certificate of Education (CSE) in two or three of the following subjects: English language, mathematics, geography, art, technical drawing, a modern language or surveying. Jobs are advertised in the newspapers, but your Youth Employment Officer should be able to advise you about where to apply. You are then trained on the job, rather like an apprenticeship.

There are two sorts of surveyors: land surveyors who measure the physical features of town and country, and hydrographic surveyors who measure and record information about seas, rivers, tides, currents and other water features. Most of these surveyors work for the government, but some work for oil companies and in other offices.

You can start to train as a surveyor at the age of sixteen if you have five GCE 'O'-Level or equivalent passes. These must include English language and mathematics. To take higher qualifications you will also need two passes at GCE Advanced Level. There are three methods of training. You can work as a paid trainee for four to five years and study part-time through correspondence courses or at a technical college for your examinations. You can take a three-year degree course in civil engineering, mathematics, physical science or geography and follow this with a postgraduate course in land surveying. You can take a CNAA (Council of National Academic Awards) degree in surveying. You cannot take your final surveying examinations until you have had four years' experience in land or hydrographic surveying.

Magpie Makes Music

Quiz compiled by Angie Errigo

Test your musical knowledge with these 50 questions.
Most people will feel more at home with some of the categories
than with others. If you do equally well in all of them, you
really are a music mastermind! But have a try at all of the
questions first, and impress your friends later with the answers to
any you may not have known before. Answers are on page 128.

General Knowledge

1 Who writes the lyrics for Elton John's music?
2 What do Abba, Brotherhood of Man and Dana have in common?
3 The daughter of television personality Bruce Forsyth is a member of which vocal group?
4 What internationally acclaimed guitarist played in the Yardbirds, John Mayall's Bluesbreakers and Cream in the 1960s?
5 Who did Pat McGlynn replace in the Bay City Rollers?
6 Who is the only English singer ever to have won a Grammy Award for Best Female Country and Western Singer?
7 For which group does Jake Hooker play lead guitar?
8 'The King' of Rock and Roll, he started his career singing numbers by black Rhythm and Blues artists— such as 'That's Alright Mama' by 'Big Boy' Arthur Crudup. Who is he?
9 Which top pop singer is managed by former pop star-turned-actor Adam Faith?
10 What does Mickie Most do in the recording business?

Blasts from the Past

11 The Rubettes' hit 'Oh Boy' was originally recorded in 1957 by which legendary pop star?
12 In which all-girl vocal group did Diana Ross sing?
13 Who wrote the most famous rock opera, 'Tommy'? Of which group is he a member?
14 The Bay City Rollers' hit 'Bye Bye Baby' first charted in 1964 for which still-popular group?
15 What black American rock and roller wrote and recorded songs later covered by the Beatles, the Rolling Stones, Rod Stewart and ELO, among others?

The Name Game

Which pop performers changed their names from the following?:
16 Paul Gadd
17 Pauline Matthews
18 Reginald Dwight
19 Lesley Hornby
20 David Jones

Musical Landmarks

21 What American city was the birthplace of famous soul record company Tamla-Motown?
22 Where was the largest outdoor music festival in British history held?
23 What city is the world's centre for Country and Western music?
24 Which island in the West Indies has produced the best-known reggae musicians?
25 Where was the Cavern club, the stepping stone to stardom for bands in the 60's Beat Boom?

Anagrams

Unscramble each line of letters to find five famous names.
26 sword treat
27 view rest done
28 cane tray clump
29 ace pool icer
30 aids ran so

The Eyes Have It

Whose peepers are these?:
31

32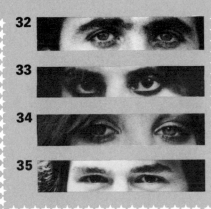

33

34

35

Music Language

36 How many notes are there in an octave?

37 What three notes make a G chord?

38 What is meant by the *tempo* of music?

39 The sign ♭ indicates that the pitch of a note is lowered one half-step. What is it called?

40 What is the distance between two notes called?

Music from Television and Films

41 Showaddywaddy first came to national attention on what TV programme?

42 Who has written and produced all of the Wombles' hit records?

43 Singer-actors David Essex and Paul Nicholas have both played Jesus Christ on the stage. Can you name the musicals in which they starred? What movie did they appear in together?

44 The theme song for the comedy series 'No Honestly' was written by which lady pop composer and singer?

45 Singer-songwriter Paul Williams wrote the film score for an all children's gangster musical. What was it?

Classical Music

46 Who wrote 'The Nutcracker Suite'?

47 Gian-Carlo Menotti wrote a lovely Christmas opera about a lame shepherd boy and the Three Kings. Can you name the opera?

48 What European capital was the birthplace of the waltz?

49 Franz Gruber wrote a well-loved Christmas carol to sing without music when his church organ broke down. What is it?

50 Who wrote 'Peter and the Wolf'?

" CAN I HELP YOU MADAM ? "

" YOU'RE NOT PASSING THE BATON QUICK ENOUGH. SO FROM NOW ON WE USE A STICK OF DYNAMITE ! "

Growing Things

FRUIT PIPS ...   DON'T THROW THOSE PIPS AWAY! IF YOU TAKE CARE YOU CAN GROW LITTLE TREES FROM THEM. THIS IS WHAT YOU'LL NEED: PIPS, FLOWER POT, NEWSPAPER, SAND, POTTING COMPOST, WATER. NOTE: WITH ORANGES, GRAPEFRUIT AND LEMONS, SOAK THE PIPS (THEY ARE THE SEEDS OF THE PLANT) OVERNIGHT BEFORE BEGINNING. WITH OTHER PIPS, SUCH AS PLUMS, PEARS AND APPLES, KEEP THEM IN A JAM JAR OF DAMP PEAT MOSS IN A REFRIGERATOR UNTIL A SHOOT APPEARS.

POTTING COMPOST

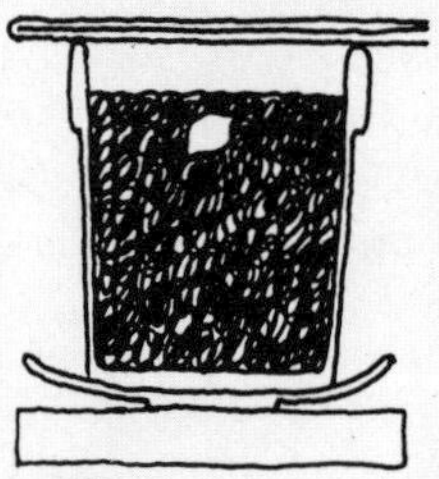

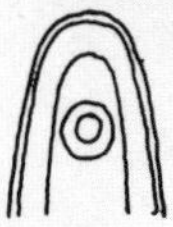

MIX A HALF AND HALF MIXTURE OF SAND AND COMPOST AND FILL THE FLOWER POT TO ABOUT 2cm.(1 in.) FROM THE TOP, PLACE THE PIP ON TOP OF THE SOIL AND COVER LIGHTLY WITH SOME MORE SOIL. PUT THE POT IN A REALLY WARM PLACE AND COVER IT WITH A SHEET OF NEWSPAPER. MAKE SURE THE SOIL DOES NOT DRY OUT - YOU MAY HAVE TO WATER IT EVERY DAY. AFTER A WHILE YOU SHOULD SEE A SHOOT APPEARING.

AVOCADO STONES...   YOU WILL NEED: AVOCADO STONE NARROW-TOPPED JAR OR EGG CUP, COMPOST, WATER, FLOWER POT. TAKE THE BROWN SKIN OFF THE STONE AND PLACE IT POINTED- -END-UP IN THE GLASS SO THAT IT IS SUSPENDED WITH THE BOTTOM IN WATER AND THE TOP OUT.

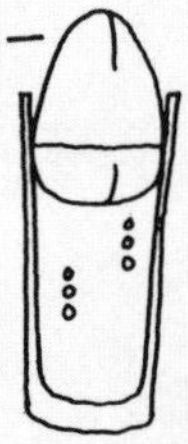

POTTING COMPOST

KEEP THE GLASS IN A DARK PLACE AT FIRST, BUT ONCE THE ROOTS HAVE STARTED TO APPEAR (PROBABLY AFTER A FEW WEEKS) BRING IT OUT INTO THE LIGHT. AFTER ABOUT EIGHT WEEKS WHEN THE PLANT HAS GROWN AND HAS A FEW LEAVES, PUT IT IN A POT WITH POTTING COMPOST. WATER REGULARLY, ALTHOUGH PLANTS ARE QUITE DIFFICULT TO GROW IN THIS WAY, SUCCESS CAN BE QUITE SPECTACULAR - AVOCADO PLANTS ARE KNOWN TO HAVE GROWN 3m. (10ft.) WHEN STARTED IN THIS WAY.

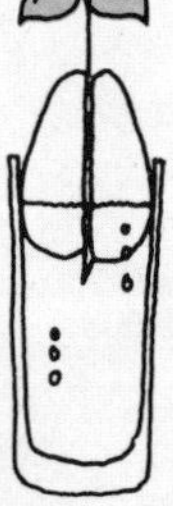

BOTTLE GARDEN YOU WILL NEED : A LARGE BOTTLE OR JAR WITH A TIGHT FITTING LID, SOME SMALL PEBBLES, A KNITTING NEEDLE WITH A CORK ON THE END, A SMALL PACKET OF GOOD POTTING COMPOST, TWO LONG STICKS, SLOW-GROWING PLANTS

POTTING COMPOST

① ONCE YOU HAVE FOUND A PRETTILY-SHAPED GLASS BOTTLE OR JAR — CONTAINERS OF BATH SALTS OR COTTON WOOL BALLS ARE IDEAL — WASH IT OUT THOROUGHLY TO GET RID OF ANY TRACES OF THE PREVIOUS CONTENTS.

② WASH THE PEBBLES AND ROLL THEM VERY GENTLY DOWN THE SIDE OF THE BOTTLE UNTIL YOU HAVE A LAYER OF PEBBLES COVERING THE BOTTOM. ③ ADD THE COMPOST USING A FUNNEL SO AS NOT TO DIRTY THE SIDES OF THE BOTTLE, FILL IT TO A DEPTH OF 10 cm. (4 in.) OR MORE IF YOU HAVE A VERY BIG BOTTLE.

④ MAKE A HOLE IN THE SOIL WITH A STICK AND LOWER A PLANT IN TO THE HOLE USING TWO STICKS. ⑤ COVER THE ROOTS OVER WITH THE COMPOST USING THE CORK ON THE KNITTING NEEDLE, AND PRESS THE SOIL GENTLY AROUND THE PLANT. REPEAT THIS PROCESS FOR ANY OTHER PLANTS YOU WANT IN YOUR BOTTLE GARDEN. DAMPEN THE SOIL WITH A LITTLE WATER AND PUT THE LID ON THE BOTTLE SO THAT IT IS AIRTIGHT. IN THIS WAY THE WATER DOES NOT EVAPORATE, AND YOU PROBABLY WON'T HAVE TO WATER THE PLANTS AGAIN FOR A YEAR.

MUSEUMS—BRINGING THE PAST TO LIFE

by Oliver Green

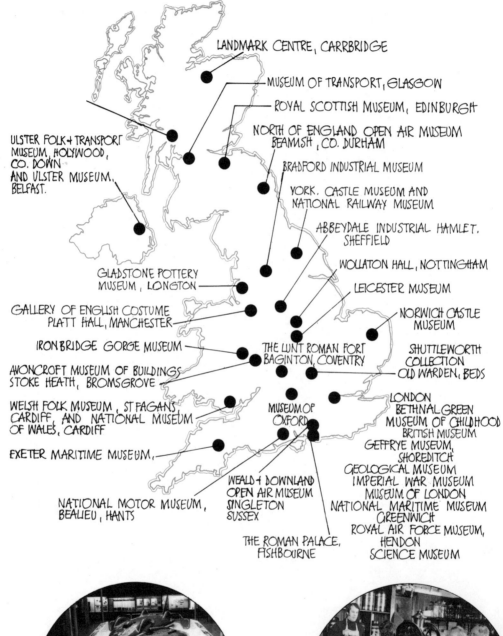

LANDMARK CENTRE, CARRBRIDGE

MUSEUM OF TRANSPORT, GLASGOW

ROYAL SCOTTISH MUSEUM, EDINBURGH

NORTH OF ENGLAND OPEN AIR MUSEUM BEAMISH, CO. DURHAM

BRADFORD INDUSTRIAL MUSEUM

YORK, CASTLE MUSEUM AND NATIONAL RAILWAY MUSEUM

ABBEYDALE INDUSTRIAL HAMLET, SHEFFIELD

WOLLATON HALL, NOTTINGHAM

LEICESTER MUSEUM

NORWICH CASTLE MUSEUM

SHUTTLEWORTH COLLECTION OLD WARDEN, BEDS

ULSTER FOLK + TRANSPORT MUSEUM, HOLYWOOD, CO. DOWN AND ULSTER MUSEUM, BELFAST.

GLADSTONE POTTERY MUSEUM, LONGTON

GALLERY OF ENGLISH COSTUME PLATT HALL, MANCHESTER

IRONBRIDGE GORGE MUSEUM

AVONCROFT MUSEUM OF BUILDINGS STOKE HEATH, BROMSGROVE

THE LUNT ROMAN FORT BAGINTON, COVENTRY

WELSH FOLK MUSEUM, ST FAGANS, CARDIFF, AND NATIONAL MUSEUM OF WALES, CARDIFF

MUSEUM OF OXFORD

LONDON
BETHNAL GREEN
MUSEUM OF CHILDHOOD
BRITISH MUSEUM
GEFFRYE MUSEUM, SHOREDITCH
GEOLOGICAL MUSEUM
IMPERIAL WAR MUSEUM
MUSEUM OF LONDON
NATIONAL MARITIME MUSEUM GREENWICH
ROYAL AIR FORCE MUSEUM, HENDON
SCIENCE MUSEUM

EXETER MARITIME MUSEUM,

NATIONAL MOTOR MUSEUM, BEAULIEU, HANTS

WEALD + DOWNLAND OPEN AIR MUSEUM SINGLETON SUSSEX

THE ROMAN PALACE, FISHBOURNE

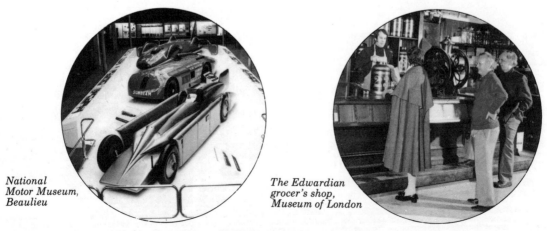

National Motor Museum, Beaulieu

The Edwardian grocer's shop, Museum of London

When did you last visit a museum? You may have been on a visit from school, but have you ever thought of going in your own time? Until a few years ago most museums were not very inviting places. The buildings were often gloomy and the displays were dull, with endless rows of remains laid out behind glass. It isn't surprising that museums have been looked upon as places where relics from the dead past just gather dust. To get rid of this old image, museums have recently begun using their collections in new ways which help bring the past to life.

When the site of an ancient settlement is discovered, broken remains are much more likely to be dug up than complete undamaged objects. But these pieces are valuable clues from which an archaeologist (an expert who studies ancient remains) can tell us a great deal about the people who used them and the way they lived. He will also know how the complete objects probably looked, but when a few remains are displayed in a museum, you and I may find this difficult to imagine. Some museums have found a way round this by displaying 'reconstructions'. Following the archaeologist's instructions and using a fragment as the starting point, the missing parts of an object can be built up with modern materials.

Reconstruction can be done on a much larger scale by rebuilding complete rooms and buildings as they once looked, based on the evidence of what little remains. At Baginton, near Coventry, a full scale Roman fort has been reconstructed on the site where the remains of the original were discovered, using, as far as possible, the same materials and methods as the Roman army. Here museums are borrowing the techniques of

Above: One of the spectacular bottle ovens in the yard of the Gladstone Pottery Museum.

television and film producers who create elaborate 'sets' for historical plays. The difference, of course, is that in films the sets and costumes are usually specially made but very accurate 'fakes', while museums are able to use genuine objects with just a few replicas to provide a realistic setting.

Sometimes it is possible to take a complete building to pieces and re-assemble it at a museum. The Castle Museum at York has a whole indoor street of old shops and houses that have been rebuilt in this way. But few museums have the space to do this inside their own buildings, and most reconstructions of this kind now take place at open air museums such as the Weald and Downland at Singleton and Avoncroft near Bromsgrove. The most ambitious project of all is Beamish Museum, where a complete coal mine is being reconstructed and there are plans to re-create a whole Victorian town with a tramway.

It is always more interesting to see the things of the past being used. Obviously many objects are too fragile for this, but at industrial museums old manufacturing processes are often demonstrated and where possible the original machinery is used. At the Gladstone Pottery Museum you can even buy the products that the craftsmen produce.

Of course, museums are usually more interested in the objects of the past, but as fashions change and technology progresses more quickly than ever before, nothing is too modern to find its way into a museum. The Science Museum has already acquired an Apollo space capsule and the proto-type Concorde. Before long many of the everyday items you are familiar with may also become museum pieces. You might like to think about which of them you would choose to give museum visitors of the future an idea of the life in the 1970s.

Above: A complete street, Kirkgate, has been reconstructed at the Castle Museum, York.

" ONE SHARK-FIN SOUP SIR. "

THAT REMINDS ME — ARE WE GOING POT-HOLING THIS WEEKEND?

LADY — THIS IS NO TIME TO PUT YOUR FEET UP!

THIS IS THE FIRST TIME YOU'VE SLEPT UNDER THE STARS AIN'T IT SON?

" YOU MEAN 'FLOOR-LESS' DON'T YOU!"

Where Would We Be Without Words... Speechless!

by Martyn Day

Did you know that you can speak a little Persian, a touch of Indian, with a smattering of Latin and Viking thrown in for good measure? Take a sentence like . . . 'my mother will go berserk because I have left her shampoo in the caravan!' It sounds simple, doesn't it . . . but if you examine the words carefully you will find that 'mother' comes from the Latin word '*mater*', 'berserk' is an old Viking term . . . ask an old Viking!, 'shampoo' comes from India, and 'caravan' is Persian. In fact many of the words that we use have strange and exotic origins, especially those which have developed from people's names. Let's look at a few:

How about your blazer? Now that takes its name from the good ship *H.M.S. Blazer*, which had a very fashion-conscious captain. He decided in 1845, that his trusty crew would look rather trendy in blue and white striped jerseys . . . and so they did, and soon the name 'blazer' was given to any brightly coloured or striped jacket.

Perhaps you have a Biro in your blazer pocket. That is named after a clever Hungarian called Lazlo Joseph Biro who got rather fed up with writing with pencils that always needed sharpening, and pens that needed ink. So he invented a special pen with a ball point that never needed sharpening or filling. When they first appeared in 1946 they cost over £2 each, but now you can buy them for as little as 5p! O.K?

Well I'm afraid that O.K is not O.K! That was started in 1839 by an American political party called 'Democratic O.K', the O.K being the initials of Old Kinderhook, the birthplace of Martin Van Buren, the Democratic candidate. His opponents however tried to suggest that Martin couldn't spell by saying that O.K stood for 'Orl Korrect'!

And now, a story. Once upon a time there lived in France a rich young acrobat called Jules Leotard. His father owned a large villa in Toulouse with an indoor swimming pool, which had huge windows to let in the light. Each window had a long cord to open them, and these dangled over the pool. One day Jules tried swinging between the cords, and so invented the Flying Trapeze! In 1859 Jules gave his first public performance to a delighted audience in Paris, and even inspired a song called 'The Daring Young Man on the Flying Trapeze'. For his performances Jules wore a tight fitting costume, very similar to those worn by acrobats and dancers today, and called . . . of course 'leotards'!

One way of ensuring immortality is to have your name used as a common word. Jenny thinks that she would like a 'Hanley' to be used for a hairstyle that never needed combing, washing or cutting, whilst Mick wants his surname 'Robertson' to be given to a car that drives and steers itself, so that he can sleep in the back on the way to the Magpie studio!

How about you? Do you fancy having *your* name given to an everlasting lollipop, or a non-melting ice cream, a 3-D television, or perhaps a remote controlled football, then there is a silent alarm clock for late risers and bottled sunshine. . . .

GET KNITTING!

by Jean Litchfield

First of all, make sure that you have all the things you will need—wool, knitting needles, pattern, tape measure, pins, scissors and a large-eyed blunt needle for sewing up. Before you start to knit. make sure that your hands are clean, and always keep your work in a polythene bag when you are not knitting.

Casting On

The easiest method of casting on is the thumb method, which gives you a firm but elastic edge. For this you start with only one needle. Make a loop about 1 metre (1 yard) from the end of the wool and slip this loop on to the needle.

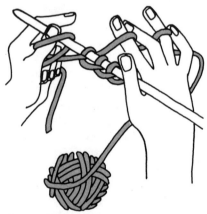

Casting On

Hold the needle in your right hand, with the main end of the wool and hold the short end of wool in your left hand. Pass the short end round your left thumb to make a loop, insert the point of the needle into this loop, pass the main wool round the point of the needle

and draw this loop through the loop on your thumb, dropping the loop off your thumb and pulling it tight (but not too tight). Repeat this process until you have the number of stitches which you will need on the needle.

The Knit Stitch

Cast on the number of stitches you need and hold the needle with the stitches on in your left hand, holding the other needle in your right hand. Keeping the wool at the back of the work, insert the point of the needle into the first stitch, pass the wool round the point of the needle and draw the loop through the stitch, dropping the stitch off the left hand needle. You have now knitted one stitch. Insert the point of the needle into the next stitch and continue in the same way until you have knitted all the stitches; turn the work round and work the next row in the same way. If you knit every row this makes a ridged fabric and is called *garter* stitch.

The Knit Stitch—Inserting the needle through the stitch

Passing the wool round the point of the needle

Drawing the loop through the stitch

The Knit Stitch Completed

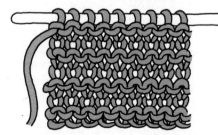

Plain Knitting or Garter Stitch

The Purl Stitch

Cast on your stitches and hold the needles as for the Knit Stitch. Keeping the wool at the front of the work, insert the point of the needle from right to left into the first stitch, take the wool round the point of the needle and back to the front, draw the loop through the stitch, dropping the stitch off the left hand needle. You have now purled one stitch. Continue in this way along the row. If you knit one row and purl one row alternately this makes a fabric which is smooth on the front and ridged on the back and is called *stocking* stitch.

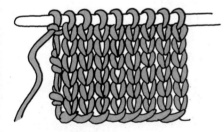

The Purl Stitch

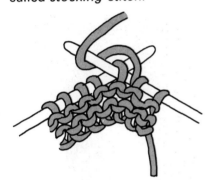

Stocking Stitch

Ribbing

This consists of some knit stitches and some purl stitches in the same row. The number can vary according to the pattern, but we will do knit one, purl one rib. Cast on your stitches as before and knit the first stitch in the row, bring the wool between the needles

to the front of the work and purl the next stitch, then take the wool between the needles to the back of the work and knit the next stitch. Continue in this way to the end of the row. On the next row, you may find that you start the row with a purl stitch, so read your pattern carefully, to be sure that you know what to do.

Decreasing

To decrease a stitch you knit two stitches together (in the pattern this is called K2 tog). Insert the point of the needle into both of the first two stitches, pass the wool round the point of the needle and knit the two stitches together as one. You have now *decreased* one stitch.

Casting off

Knit the first two stitches of the row as for ordinary Knit stitches, then with the point of the left hand needle, lift the first stitch over the second stitch and off the needle, leaving one stitch on the right hand needle. Knit the next stitch, then pass the first stitch over this one. Continue in this way until only one stitch remains on the right hand needle, then break off the wool and pull the end through the stitch on the needle and draw it up firmly.

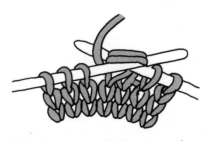

Knitting two stitches together

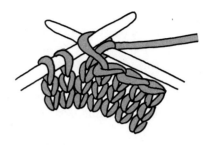

Casting off

Tension

When you have practised the basic stitches, you will want to start to make something. To be sure that this is the right size you must learn about tension. This means the number of stitches and rows in a given measurement. On the scarf we have 11 stitches and 15 rows to 5cm (2in). Using 4mm (No. 8) needles cast on 11 stitches and work in stocking stitch for 15 rows, then cast off. Place this square flat on the table and measure it—it should measure 5cm in each direction. If it is too big, start again with a smaller needle, 3¾mm (No. 9); if it is too small, try with a larger needle, 4½mm (No. 7). When you are sure that your square is the right size you can start to make your scarf, using the size of needles you needed to make your square right.

Joining the wool

When you are knitting with different colours, or when you come to the end of a ball of wool, always join in the new ball at the beginning of a row. Break off the colour you have been using, leaving an end of about 8cm (3in). Take the new colour and leaving an end of this about 8cm again, knot this to the first colour as near to the work as possible, then carry on knitting with this colour. When you have finished the work, darn the ends in neatly on the wrong side of the work.

Pressing and Sewing Up

When you have finished your scarf, lay it right side downwards on an ironing board, or on a table padded with a thick blanket and covered with a sheet. Measure the width and length and pin it carefully all round, using one pin about every 1cm ($\frac{1}{2}$in). Wring out a cloth in water, lay this over the work, then using the iron set at 'wool' press the work all over. Do not run the iron up and down the work or it will stretch it, lift it up and place down on the next bit until you have pressed the scarf all over. When it is all pressed, leave it for a little while to dry, then take out the pins. To join a seam, thread the wool into a large-eyed blunt needle (called a tapestry needle) and hold the two edges together. Make a small back stitch to start with, so that it will not come undone, then take a loop from each side of the seam alternately, taking care not to pull your sewing too tightly. When the seam is done it should be able to stretch in the same way as the knitting.

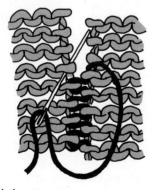

Joining a seam

Pom-Pon

To make a pom-pon cut two circles of card the size of the pom-pon—for the cap this will be 5cm (2in), then cut a hole in the centre of each circle. Place the two circles together and wind the wool over the card, up through the centre hole and back over the side until the centre hole is full up. Cut round the edge of the pom-pon between the two pieces of card. Tie a length of wool very firmly round the pom-pon between the two pieces of card, then cut the card away and trim the pom-pon to make it an even shape.

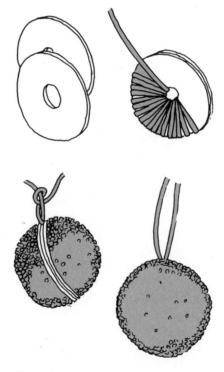

Pom-Pon

Fringe

To make a fringe, cut a piece of cardboard slightly wider than the length you want your fringe to be. If you want a fringe to measure 7cm (2$\frac{3}{4}$in) cut your card 7.5cm (3in) wide.

Wind the wool round and round the card until you have as many pieces as you want, then cut along one side of the card. This will give you pieces of wool 15cm (6in) long. Take two pieces, or as many as you want for each knot, and fold them in half. Using a crochet hook, insert the hook through the edge of the work, place the loops of your fringe over the hook and draw through the work. Pull this loop up a bit so that you can pass the ends of the fringe through, then pull the ends of the fringe tight. Repeat this along the edge of the work, spacing the knots evenly.

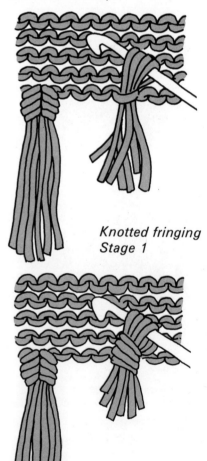

Knotted fringing Stage 1

Stage 2

PATTERN FOR A SCARF AND CAP

MATERIALS 3 balls each of A, E, 4 balls each of B, C, D totalling 18.
Scarf 25gr balls of Emu Scotch Superwash Double Knitting in each of 5 colours, coded A, B, C, D and E.
Cap 1 ball in each of the 5 colours.
1 pair of 4mm (No. 8) Knitting needles.

Measurements
Scarf 30cm wide and 245cm long (approx 12 in wide and 98in long). Cap to fit approx 9–12 years.

Tension
11 sts and 15 rows to 5cm (2in) measured over st st on 4mm needles.

Abbreviations
K – knit; P – purl; sts – stitches; st st – stocking stitch; rep – repeat; tog – together; cm – centimetres; in – inches.

Scarf
With 4mm needles and A cast on 66 sts and work in st st, working * 5cm (2in) each in A, B, C, D, E, D, C and B. Rep from * 5 times more, then work 5cm (2in) in A. Cast off.

To Make Up
Pin work out to size and press on the wrong side with a warm iron over a damp cloth. If you like, join the sides of the scarf in one long seam to make the work into a tube. Cut the remaining yarn into lengths of 16cm (12in) and using one colour or all the colours as you wish, make a knotted fringe along each end of scarf. Trim fringe.

Cap
With 4mm needles and A cast on 109 sts.
1st row K1, * P1, K1, rep from * to end.
2nd row P1, * K1, P1, rep from * to end.
Rep these 2 rows 3 times more.
Continue in the same rib, work 8 rows each in B, C, D, E, D, C and B.
Shape Top (using A).
1st row * K4, K2 tog, rep from * to last st, K1.
2nd row and every alternate row P to end.
3rd row * K3, K2 tog, rep from * to last st, K1.
5th row * K2, K2 tog, rep from * to last st, K1.

7th row * K1, K2 tog, rep from * to last st, K1.
9th row * K2 tog, rep from * to last st, K1.
10th row P to end.
Break off wool, leaving an end about 30cm (12in) long. Using a big darning needle, thread the end of the wool through the 27sts on the needle, draw up tightly and fasten off. Using the same end of wool, join the seam neatly. Do not press the work or you will flatten the rib. Make a pom-pon approx 5cm (2in) across and sew to top of cap.

Nature Trail Through the Park

by Dr Pat Morris

The black-headed gull with its summer plumage.

Ragwort growing out of a wall.

A dandelion clock.

A horse chestnut bud.

A pair of mallards, the female is diving.

A tufted duck.

Most of us think that wild animals and exciting Natural History are things that can only be seen in the countryside or on television. Actually, there's lots to be seen, even in the most ordinary town park. You have to know what to look for of course, and it all becomes much more interesting if you understand some of the details that many people just don't know about.

The easiest animals to see are the birds. Few parks have less than a dozen different kinds and if there is a pond, you should be able to find at least 15 sorts of birds. Why not try? Make a list of them. Did you know that over 50 different species of birds are regularly seen each year in the parks of Central London, including owls and even hawks?

Seagulls regularly visit parks and recreation grounds, especially in the winter. People think they only come inland when the weather is bad at sea, but in fact many gulls have found that it's easier to find food in a park or on a rubbish tip than it is at the coast and they probably only go back to the seaside in order to nest. Watch them, some seem to have learnt the trick of stamping about on wet ground to encourage worms to come to the surface to be eaten. There are four species of gull you are likely to see, but the commonest, and smallest, is the black-headed gull. This has a red beak and legs to distinguish it from other gulls but in winter (the time you are most likely to see it) it has no black head! This can be very confusing to people who don't know about gulls. Actually the dark chocolate brown feathers on the head are lost in the Autumn and only a little dark patch remains behind the eye until the deep brown (not really black) hood is grown again in Spring.

Right: 1 the black-headed gull, 2 the greater black-backed gull, 3 the herring gull, 4 the lesser black-backed gull.

Another common park bird that clearly changes its dress with the season is the ordinary mallard duck. Actually it shows most clearly in the drake (the name given to males of the duck family). Mallard drakes are mostly pale grey and have glossy green heads, whereas their wives, the ducks, are brown all over (look for the smart curly black tail feathers in the drake—does the duck have them too?) However, in the summer, all the ducks and drakes look more or less the same. They are dull brown, you just don't see glossy green heads in summer. When did the change take place? That is another date to note in your diary. You will see, soon after Easter that the drakes gradually, over a period of a few weeks, lose their glossy head feathers and go dull brown on the head and body. The reason is that their smart feathers are really only there to show off during the breeding season. The rest of the year there is no need to impress the ducks so they might as well be a dull colour and less easy to see. Ducks are brown, partly because they need to be well camouflaged when they are sitting on their eggs. These may be laid in almost any month of the year—when did you see the first brood of ducklings and how many were there? Notice how the families are large when the ducklings first hatch, but many die or are killed by predators, so that the larger (older) ducklings form smaller families. Notice too how their fluffy yellow and brown down is soon replaced by the growth of proper feathers.

Other ducks may come to your park, or perhaps a few colourful foreign ones are kept as ornaments. One winter visitor is the tufted duck; a chubby black fellow with a big white patch on the side. This species migrates, just as swallows and cuckoos leave Britain and spend the winter in sunny Africa, so tufted ducks come to Britain because our winter, nasty though it may be, is still much warmer than where they normally live. Many of the tufted ducks in our parks will have been born (or hatched) in Eastern Europe, and some of those that spend winter in London's St James's Park go home in Spring to places as far away as Siberia.

Ducks eat bread of course but that is not their natural food. Tufted ducks prefer worms dug out of the mud, mallard eat water plants. Both will feed on the bottom of the pond, but notice how differently they feed. The mallard will 'up-end' sticking its bottom in the air and poking about underwater with its beak. Tufted ducks can dive instead, staying underwater for a long time (time the dives by counting slowly), mallards cannot. Their diving ability allows 'tufties' to live in deep water, yet still feed on the bottom; whereas mallards feed mainly in the shallows where they can reach the bottom by 'up-ending' and stretching out their neck.

There are many other details to look for in our town birds. See how the male house sparrow's black bib becomes bigger in summer; how starlings have yellow beaks in spring and black ones in autumn, how a coot has a different kind of webbed foot to a duck, yet both live in water.

Birds are not the only inhabitants of your local park, there are probably some furry mammals too. The trouble is that mice, shrews, hedgehogs and the like all tend to hide but you should see squirrels, especially in the early morning. It is the grey squirrel that you will see in the park. It was introduced to Britain at the turn of the century. Some were brought from the United States and released in a few of the London parks. From there, in a mere 70 years or so they have spread and colonised most of mainland Britain. They have replaced the red squirrel which has now gone from most places and anyway does not usually live in towns and gardens. People often *think* they have seen red squirrels in parks because they do not realise that grey squirrels go very brown during the late summer and may then be wrongly identified. Notice how squirrels feed using their hands. Not many animals do this, how many others can you think of? Look carefully at the litter left behind after a squirrel's meal. The way it eats pine cones is particularly characteristic, pulling the prongs off the cone to get the seeds out, and throwing away a chewed pine cone core the way we discard an apple core. Look for these chewed cones as evidence that squirrels **are** about even if you cannot see them. Watch how squirrels remove the shells from peanuts and see the big tooth marks left in a half-chewed conker! People often say that squirrels hibernate in winter. You can prove them wrong by noting in your diary all the squirrels seen over the Christmas holidays. Look for their footprints if there is any snow about. Actually squirrels are active on fine days throughout the winter, but they become sleepy and sluggish when the weather is cold and wet. On such days as this they sensibly stay in bed!

The grey squirrel, introduced to Britain from America.

Plants are interesting too. Find a horse chestnut tree. It has big brown sticky buds in early spring (sticky to keep insects from damaging the buds). These burst into the young leaves when the fine weather comes. Note the date in your diary and ask your friends or relatives who live more than 100 miles away if their sticky buds have opened yet—they should do so earlier in southern areas than in the colder north. (They open earlier in town parks than in the countryside too, because towns tend to be a little warmer than the surrounding country—check with your friends or on a day's outing.) Later in the year the horse chestnut bears tall white cones of pretty flowers, looking like candles on the tree; (when do they appear, how long do they last?) Both are again affected by where the tree grows, and later still it produces conkers, each one in a spiky shell.

How many kinds of tree are in your park? Collect the fallen leaves and identify them, match them up with the appropriate nuts or seeds.

Most park keepers mow their grass, look for patches the mower has missed and see what the grass *should* look like if it's left alone. See how different grasses have different seed and flower heads. Some look just like wheat or barley because the farmer's corn is really only a special kind of grass. Look at mown grass, see how the leaf tips are chopped off and notice how few plants can live in a mown patch because few plants other than grass can put up with being regularly mown. On waste ground you will see things like thistles, dandelions and rosebay willow herb. They are able to travel easily and quickly to new growing places because they have delicate 'parachute' seeds that are dispersed by the wind. Collect some, use a magnifying glass to examine the beautiful structure of a dandelion 'clock' or seed head. In what months do you find them? Even stinging nettles can be interesting. Have you noticed they have square stems? Nettles are the favourite food plant for caterpillars of the peacock and pretty tortoiseshell butterflies, so we should not clear away all these 'weeds' or we will have lost our butterflies.

So there is much to see and do, even in the most ordinary place. Next time you visit your park, look carefully at what you see, notice that different types of tree have different branching patterns and different barks, not just different leaves. Imagine you were a patch of grass. Think of all the problems that lawn grass has to face when you run about on it!

ALL THE FUN OF THE FAIR

by Kate Marlow

Before departure, to ensure that the birds arrived in perfect condition after their long trek, their feet were dipped in a mixture of sand and tar. There is no record, however, of any protection being available for the poor drovers' feet.

Geese were not the only commodities sold at the great market, many fine cheeses, clothing, boots and goods to stock up the larder for the whole winter were on sale too. Some of the goods were brought in specially from other areas of the country, and would not be available again until the following year's fair.

The fair held in 1766 was more notorious than most since. Prospective cheese customers were outraged and infuriated by the fact that the farmers had increased the price of cheese. Cheeses, the like of which had cost twenty-five shillings, (£1.25 in our present money) the previous year, were priced at thirty shillings (£1.50). These were not the prices for a pound, but a hundredweight! The same quantity of cheddar cheese today, would cost about £70. The angry customers of 1766 were not, as we are today, so used to accepting

Nottingham has many claims to fame, amongst them the beautiful lace it manufactures, famous sons such as Robin Hood, D H Lawrence and the chemist Jesse Boot, and supposedly a higher ratio of women to men than any other British city. There is also a unique autumn event known as The Goosefair.

The Goosefair is the largest three-day fair in the country, covering about six hectares of parkland. It is held during the first week-end in October. Visitors are offered 'all the fun of the fair' on literally hundreds of rides, stalls and games—but there is not one single goose to be found!

More than six hundred years ago however, it was a very different story. The fair was originally a huge market, for the sale of thousands of fatted geese, which reached their prime just at this time. The geese were driven to Nottingham from as far away as the Lincolnshire Fens, and far-distant fields of Norfolk, which could have been more than one hundred miles. Because there was no alternative transport, these journeys had to be made on foot.

the years passed and transport improved, especially with the arrival of the railways, goods could be taken more easily from one part of the country to another. This meant that the very reason for the fair's existence—to stock up with goods—declined. People could now buy most of their goods all year round. This did not mean the end of the Goosefair—far from it.

By the early 1900s the fair was jammed full of shows, stalls, bazaars, cages of wild beasts, theatrical dwarfs, riding machines, and thousands of people enjoying themselves. The traders had been pushed to the edge of the market square, and the only geese to be offered for sale were toy ones. The fair now existed to give fun, fun, and more fun.

big price increases and they certainly showed their feelings.

Stalls were ransacked, huge cheeses rolled down the streets, and customers and stall-holders fought. Total chaos reigned throughout the market square. The outcome was that that winter, many people enjoyed the totally free cheese they had found in the street. Perhaps we could learn a lesson from this piece of history!

The old fairs were places where people met friends and relations they perhaps hadn't seen for a year. It's not surprising therefore, that they became places of merriment and festivity, and that from a very early date, shows were brought to the fair to entertain the people who had originally gathered for trade.

By the 1800s there were many shows, displaying many weird and wonderful sights, some of them totally new to their audiences. Without good transport few people had had an opportunity to see such 'curiosities' as Madam Tussaud's life-size waxworks, which appeared at the fair for the first time in 1819. Performing fleas, and 'wild beasts' such as real live lions and bears were on show! Unfortunate people, and animals, who were deformed in some way, or simply over- or under-sized, were 'displayed' for people to gawp at. It was probably at a fair too, where people saw their first bioscope show. These were early picture shows, and the beginnings of the world of cinema.

In 1885 Twigdon's Riding Machine arrived. This was the first roundabout to appear at the Goosefair. It consisted of model horses which were mounted on a circular platform that was pushed round by hand! The fair attracted more and more people and, as

People spent a lot of money at the fair, money they had saved during the previous weeks and months. In 1899 it cost one shilling, or five pence, for an adult to enter Wombell's Menagerie. Nottingham's children received and came to expect, not only a birthday and Christmas present, but a Goosefair present too.

In 1928, the people of Nottingham heard a startling piece of news—the Goosefair could not be held any longer. Because tram lines were being laid, it had to move from the market square. In 1929, however, the fair did open as usual, but on a new site 1½ miles away.

Since its move, the only link with a market has been the sale of sheep and horses before the fair opens. This takes place several miles away at the city's Cattle Market, but now, sadly, this appears to be lacking public support. Considering that the city of Nottingham has a population of about 300,000

such 'torture' on a ride, you have to invest 15 or 20 pence and sometimes wait your turn in a queue of up to 150 half-terrified, half-excited fairgoers.

If you don't have a head for heights, and decide that the Big Wheel and the Dive Bomber are not for you, and that you don't have the stomach for the Waltzer or Skid, there are gentler amusements available. There are traditional Galloping Horses, and a Victorian Cake-Walk, or you can test your skills, instead of your endurance. There are prizes to be won at the Rifle Range, the Hoopla stall, the Coconut Shy or at a game of Bingo.

Parents have little choice as to whether they will visit the fair—children make quite sure of that. Local schools close for the Friday afternoon, for

people, and that the fair attracts about 500,000 people, the same cannot be said about the main event!

At noon, on the first Thursday in October, the fair is opened with a short ceremony led by the Lord Mayor, the Sheriff of Nottingham, and other civic dignitaries. But that's the end of formality. The minute the mayor has rung the silver bells, the stalls are illuminated, the music starts, and the fair bursts into life. The hustle, bustle and constant noise, builds from that moment onwards. Droves of people, from every walk of life and age group, pour on to the fairground with one common aim—to enjoy themselves. By 8.00 p.m. the crush has to be seen to be believed!

Standing at any point in the fair, your eardrums are treated to a medley of at least ten different tunes, from 'Rock Around the Clock', to 'Viva Espana' beating out on a traditional fairground organ. Over and above all else, piercing screams can be heard coming from terrified, but thrilled teenagers, on the many whizzing, swirling rides.

Your nose is made to work overtime too. During a five minute stroll, it will encounter a mixture of aromas arising from sweet and sugary candyfloss, pungent onion-flavoured hot dogs, caramelised toffee apples, and the homely smell of times gone by as mushy peas simmer on coke-fired braziers. The only way in which your eyes will feast themselves upon such a spectacle again, is by making a future visit to the fair.

Just what drives people not only to frighten themselves into hysterical giggles, screams of fear and delight, but also to pay for the 'ordeal', we'll probably never know. But in order to treat yourself to

youngsters to make their pilgrimage. Coloured, candy lollipops known as 'Cocks on Sticks' are the nearest thing to geese the fair now has to offer. Other popular novelties on sale are fairy dolls, hairy spiders and bows and arrows.

From noon on Friday, until midnight on Saturday, when the Fair closes down, half a million people from Nottingham and other cities, keep the showmen working flat-out. When the lights go out, the generators are turned off and the music dies, the work is far from finished for the showmen and their men. It continues through the night; the machines which arrived less than a week before are dismantled. Racing against the clock, the showmen often hope to re-open at Hull's great fair, less than 48 hours later. By Monday afternoon all but a few people have left, by Tuesday it's all over for another year.

Bridget's Hat

by Joan Aiken

Once a twin brother and sister called Solomon and
Bridget lived together in a little tumbledown house
on the edge of a town. Bridget worked hard to earn
their food by sewing: she made dresses and hats,
petticoats and curtains, shirts and skirts and
babies' clothes for all the ladies of the town.
Solomon never did anything; he lay out in the long
grass at the back of their little house all day long,
sunning himself and sleeping, snoring when he
was asleep, alternately singing and chewing grass
blades when he was awake. He liked to dress
handsomely, so Bridget had bought him a pair of
blue velvet trousers with silver studs down the
seams, and a lilac-and-green shirt, and a pair of
grey antelope-skin boots.

Bridget herself went barefoot, for they really had
very little money, and she wore an old grey cotton
dress that one of her ladies had passed on to her
when it was almost worn out. But she did have a
beautiful hat. The crown and the wide brim were
made of skyblue silk taffeta, cunningly banded and
lapped, and decorated with a big pink velvet rose;
the inside of the wide brim was all lined with grey
furry moleskin; and the hat tied under her chin
with two dove-grey ribbons.

Bridget had made the hat for a lady in the town
whose mother died on the very day the hat was
delivered.

'I shall have to wear black for at least a year,'
sighed the lady.

'And by that time wide brims will be quite out
of fashion. You had better keep the hat for
yourself, Bridget, and make me a black one
instead.'

'What luck,' said Solomon when he heard this.
'You can sell that hat for a lot of money. I need
some new boots; nobody wears this kind any more.'

But Bridget was so fond of the hat, which had

cost her hours of work, that she could not bear to
sell it to anybody else; so she kept it herself and
promised to save up as fast as she could for
Solomon's new boots. Solomon was annoyed about
this for as long as his lazy nature would be
bothered, which was not more than a few weeks.
After that he did not mention the matter more than
once or twice a day. Bridget meant to keep the hat
for best, but the wide brim was so comfortable that
she wore it to shade her from the sun when she had
to walk a long way from home, collecting orders or
delivering dresses to her ladies. Besides, the hat
was a good advertisement of her work, and suited
her fair hair and blue eyes, though it did not go so
well with the torn old cotton dress and bare feet.

One hot summer morning Bridget was eating her
porridge on the back step of their house before
walking a long way across the town to collect an
order from the Queen of the land. For Bridget's
stitches were so small, and her notions about
colours and materials were so clever, and her
prices were so low, that all the best ladies,
including the queen herself, employed her.

She was eating her porridge fast and quietly,
because her brother Solomon was still asleep inside
the house, and she didn't want to wake him in case
he again suggested selling her hat, when a very
large grasshopper jumped slap into the middle of
her porridge bowl.

'Oh dear,' said Bridget, and she quickly spooned
the grasshopper out of the porridge, and dipped a
dipper of water from the well, and washed the
grasshopper, and set him to dry in the sun.

All the other grasshoppers round about, of which
there were a great number, had fallen silent after
the accident, but now they began chirping again.
And the grasshopper she had rescued—who was
indeed a very large one, quite the biggest she had

B.
Jane
Johnstone **121**

to the other side of the town.

'A very good wish,' said the grasshopper. 'I was thinking the same thing myself, and as I see you also need a pair of shoes, we will combine the two items.'

Bridget's bare feet, on the hot boards of the back steps, suddenly felt quite different, quite cool and comfortable. Looking down in surprise, she saw that she had on a pair of soft, elegant black suede boots, fitting up to the ankle; each boot was fastened with a diamond the size of a cherry.

She began to say thank you, but the grasshopper interrupted her.

'Now,' he said. 'Pay careful attention. The diamond that fastens your right-hand boot is a very old and precious one; it is called the Eye of the Desert, and has the power to take you wherever you want to go, if you step out with your right foot first, and wish at the same time. Is that clear? But the stone on the left boot does not have the same power—in fact I am not sure what its nature is at all, since it had to be obtained at such short notice—so on no account *ever* step out with your *left* foot while wishing, or something might go wrong. Do you understand?'

'Yes thank you, your Majesty,' said Bridget, curtseying. 'And may I say how obliged I am for your trouble. Now, if you'll excuse me, I must hurry, or I'll be late.'

And leaving her share of porridge for Solomon she clapped her hat on her head, tied its ribbons under her chin, and stepped off the back step with her right foot, saying at the same time,

'I wish to go to the Queen's palace.'

It was lucky she had tied the ribbons tight, for in one swift running step she went right across the town, and found herself, rather breathless, standing in the palace courtyard.

No one seemed surprised at her sudden arrival, though. The guards, footmen, butler, maids, pageboys and secretaries were all running about in a very distracted way, so, as Bridget had been there plenty of times before and knew her way, she walked straight through to the Queen's private parlour, where she found the Queen crying over a breakfast of melon, hot rolls, honey, and pineapple juice.

'What is the matter, your Majesty?' said Bridget in surprise, for it looked like a very nice breakfast. She still felt extremely hungry herself.

'Oh, my dear Bridget!' wept the Queen. 'Puss is missing! We think he must have been catnapped by that wretched dragon who lives out in the

ever seen—carefully waved all his legs and whiskers, and felt himself over to make sure that no stickiness remained from the porridge.

Then he turned and bowed deeply to Bridget, sweeping his whiskers right down to the ground.

'I am greatly obliged to you, my dear young lady,' he said. 'To drown in porridge would be a dreadfully undignified end for the King of the Grasshoppers.'

'Is that what you are?' said Bridget, wondering if it would seem disrespectful to eat up the porridge that he had sat in, for she had a long walk ahead of her, and was still very hungry, and the only other food in the house was Solomon's plate of porridge.

'Certainly I am the King of the Grasshoppers. And, as a small mark of my gratitude I now intend to give you a present. What shall it be?'

'Oh my gracious,' said Bridget. 'Thank your Majesty. I really don't know what to say.'

This was true; firstly because she needed so many things, and secondly because she was not sure what the grasshopper would be able to give her and did not want to hurt his feelings. Perhaps she could ask for a leaf? Or a blade of grass?

'Come, come,' said the grasshopper. 'What do you wish for most?'

'I wish I could jump about as quickly as your Majesty,' Bridget said politely, thinking of the long hot walk through dusty tarry streets, right across

desert somewhere. Not a soul has seen him since
last night, he usually comes for his breakfast long
before this and it was kidneys today, his favourite
—and the palace baker said that when he happened
to look out at dawn he saw the dragon fly past
holding something black in his claws. And *nobody*
knows where the dragon has his nest, one could go
on searching about that great dusty desert for
years—how shall I ever get on without dear
Pussums?'

'Don't worry, your Majesty,' said Bridget kindly,
seeing that this was no time to ask for payment for
a green silk petticoat embroidered with snowdrops,
'I'll have a hunt round and see if I can't find your
Pussy. Perhaps things aren't as bad as you think.'

She left the Queen's parlour and, stepping out
into the palace courtyard on to her right foot, said,

'I wish to go where the Queen's cat is.'

Although it was a hot day, the speed with which
she flew across the countryside quite cooled her
down. She crossed fields, woods, hills, and the
burnt, brown desert.

Then she came to the foot of a cliff, which was
where the dragon had his nest. There he lay, in a
big round shallow hole, something like the crater
of a volcano. Some birds line their nests with fluff.
The dragon had lined his nest with gold coins,
thick as the pebbles on a beach. In the middle was
a blue, blue pool and beside it grew a huge
rose-tree, all covered with pink roses. And under
the rose-tree lay the dragon, fast asleep, or *almost*
fast asleep, and near by, looking very sulky, but

purring as loudly as possible, sat the Queen's
black cat.

'What a bit of luck that the dragon didn't eat
him right away; keeping him for supper, I suppose,'
thought Bridget, and in a whisper she called,

'Here, puss, puss, puss! Come, pussy, pussy,
pussy!' for she did not wish to venture any closer
to the dragon in case she woke him.

The Queen's cat stuck his tail up in the air and
came galloping over to Bridget. Unfortunately he
stopped purring, and this woke the dragon, for it
was the sound of purring that had lulled him to
sleep; directly it stopped he became fidgety.

He opened his eyes and reared his great head up
into the air, so that he looked like a very large
question-mark.

Bridget crouched down on the ground, thinking
that her last minute had come. But because of her
big blue hat, which hid her completely, the dragon,
who was rather short-sighted, never saw her at all.
He thought the hat was a bit of the blue pool, with
a pink rose floating on it. The Queen's cat hastily
started purring again and the dragon, after a sharp
look all round, tucked his head under his shining
wing and went back to sleep.

Bridget instantly snatched up the cat and,
stepping out with her right foot, cried,

'I wish to be back at the palace!'

At the sound of her voice the dragon opened his
eyes again, but now Bridget was a long way off;
against the sky all the dragon could see was her
grey dress and the grey lining of her hat, which he

took to be no more than a small cloud.

He flew off to hunt for the escaped cat, but he flew off in the wrong direction.

In no time at all Bridget was back at the palace, where the Queen was so glad to have her cat returned that she could think of nothing else but giving him his breakfast and washing the sand off his paws. She told Bridget to come back another day about the petticoat.

So Bridget wished herself home again, stepping out on her right foot.

Back at home, she found that Solomon had woken up, and was just finishing her bowl of porridge, having eaten his own already.

The first thing he said was,

'Where did you get those boots?'

'Aren't they lovely?' said Bridget. 'The king of the grasshoppers gave them to me. They are wishing boots; they take you wherever you want to go.'

She slipped them off her feet, for even the best new boots make your feet a little tired when you have been wearing them for an hour or two, and, besides, Bridget was used to going barefoot all the time.

As she took them off, she noticed that a couple of gold coins from the dragon's hoard were sticking to the sole of the right boot.

'*That's* a piece of luck,' she said. 'The Queen hasn't paid me for her petticoat yet, and I didn't like to remind her. I'll just run down to the corner shop with these and buy something for dinner.'

She took the money and ran down the road barefoot, leaving her boots on the back step.

Directly she was out of sight, Solomon tried on the boots. They fitted him excellently, for, being Bridget's twin, he had feet exactly the same size.

'What a good thing we are twins,' thought Solomon. 'These boots go much better with my blue velvet trousers than those old antelope ones. And it's handy that they are wishing boots, too.'

He said aloud, 'I wish to go to the place where Bridget picked up those gold coins,' stepping out at the same time on to his left foot.

All the grasshoppers stopped their chirping and watched him whizz away.

The boots took him directly to the dragon's nest, and set him down by the blue pool. Then they melted from his feet like black wax, and that was the end of them. The two diamonds rolled into the dragon's hoard, where they still are.

The dragon woke up—he had come home very tired and peevish after hunting all over the desert for the Queen's cat and not finding it—and he was not particularly pleased to find Solomon in his nest. But he put him to work: he made Solomon sing him to sleep; and every time Solomon stopped singing the dragon opened his large red eyes and snapped, 'Go on! I wasn't asleep!'

Solomon soon became hoarse, and very tired of singing but the boots were gone and there was no way to escape; he had to make the best of things.

Meanwhile when Bridget got back from the grocer's and found both Solomon and the boots missing, she became very anxious. But she had not been worrying for long when a carriage pulled up at the door, and the white-winged coachman gave her a note in the Queen's writing:

'My dear Bridget, As a reward for finding Puss, would you like to come and live here and be our Court Dressmaker? If so, please get into the carriage and come back at once.'

'Oh dear,' thought Bridget, 'but what about Solomon?'

At that moment the King of the Grasshoppers jumped on to her shoulder.

'Don't trouble yourself about Solomon, my dear Bridget,' he told her.

'Oh, your Majesty! Is he all right? I'm afraid he may have gone off in the boots you gave me and I hadn't warned him about them.'

'He is quite all right. He has found exactly the right job,' said the King of the Grasshoppers. 'And to tell you the truth, we are very pleased to be rid of him here, for he was eating all our grass blades and quite drowned our voices with his snoring. Now goodbye, my dear Bridget; enjoy yourself at the Palace.'

So Bridget put on her beautiful hat and rode off in the carriage. As she drove through the town the Mayor's son, looking out of his window, saw her and fell bang in love with her. Three weeks later he proposed to her, she accepted, they were married, and lived happily ever after.

But even after she got married she went on making hats and petticoats and handkerchiefs for the Queen, and for her own friends, because she enjoyed making things and did it so well.

As for Solomon, he soon found out that the dragon could be put to sleep by the sound of snoring even more easily than by the sound of singing (if the truth be known the dragon preferred Solomon's snores to his songs) and so for the rest of their days they lay side by side, fast asleep, on the edge of the blue pool, under the great rose-tree with its pink blossoms.

This story (© Joan Aiken) also appears in 'Tale of a One-way Street' published by Jonathan Cape.

A DOOR TO BE FRAMED

by Danielle Sacher

SOME IDEAS FOR TRANSFORMING THE INSIDE OF YOUR BEDROOM DOOR. A WORD OF WARNING, ASK YOUR PARENTS BEFORE YOU START USING GLUE OR SELLOTAPE!

PANELLED DOORS (1-3)

CUT OUT THE SHAPE OF A MAN IN BROWN PAPER, AND WITH A FELT-TIP DRAW ARROWS ALL OVER HIS SUIT TO SHOW THAT HE IS A PRISONER. WITH PINK PAPER MAKE HIS FACE AND HANDS AND USE BLACK PAPER TO MAKE HIS FEET. DRAW EYES, NOSE AND MOUTH ONTO HIS FACE. USING WALLPAPER PASTE OR GLUE STICK HIM TO THE DOOR AND CUT AWAY WHERE THE PANELS ARE, TO MAKE HIM LOOK AS THOUGH HE IS BEHIND BARS.

USING LOTS OF DIFFERENT COLOURED PAPER MAKE A HUGE PLANT IN A POT, STICK IT ON THE DOOR AND ONCE AGAIN CUT AWAY WHERE THE DOOR PANELS COME.

CUT OUT OBLONGS OF WALLPAPER, WRAPPING PAPER OR HESSIAN TO FIT THE PANELS IN YOUR DOOR. STICK THEM NEATLY ON TO THE PANELS USING GLUE OR WALLPAPER PASTE. TRIM THE EDGE USING BRAID OR STICKY TAPE.

FLUSH DOORS (4-5)

MAKE AN ENORMOUS FACE USING THICK BROWN WOOL FOR THE NOSE, EYEBROWS AND EYELASHES. CUT OUT SHAPES OF BRIGHTLY-COLOURED PAPER FOR THE MOUTH AND CHEEKS.

GIVE YOUR DOOR PANELS WITH STRIPS OF COLOURED SELLOTAPE. IF YOU USE A SECOND STRIP IN A DARK COLOUR YOU WILL CREATE AN IMPRESSION OF DEPTH. LOOK AT THE HINGES ON AN OLD GATE OR CHURCH DOOR AND MAKE SOME IN PAPER

How Many Magpie Badges Have You Got?

These are the Magpie Badges. You could own ten of them. Each one means that you have done something special. So why not see how many you can collect? This is what you have to do to get each badge.

The Original Magpie Badge
This badge is only given for an especially good letter or drawing or anything which has taken much more time and trouble than usual to complete. You cannot ask for this badge.

One for Sorrow
If you have spent one night or more in hospital, let Magpie know and ask your nurse or doctor or your parents to sign the letter.

Two for Joy
When you have passed any sort of test or examination, write Magpie a letter and ask your teacher to sign it.

Three for a Girl and Four for a Boy
These badges are given to girls or boys who write an interesting letter to Magpie on any subject they choose. A good drawing or painting can also qualify for these badges.

Five for Silver
This is a very special badge. You are given it if you send in a really original idea for a Magpie programme item. Write in detail about how you think the item should be arranged for the programme, and if Magpie likes the idea, you will have earned the badge.

Six for Gold
All you have to do to qualify for this badge is send Magpie a tall story, preferably of your own invention.

Seven for a Secret Never to be Told
If you think that one of your friends has done a good deed, write and tell Magpie, giving your friend's name and address, and they will be sent the badge. You cannot nominate yourself, but if you have done a good deed you can always qualify for the badge by asking a friend to write about the deed to Magpie.

Eight for a Wish
All runners up in Magpie competitions receive this badge.

Nine for a Kiss
Jenny gives this badge to any boy or girl who has learnt to swim since 1 July 1972. Your letter should be signed by your parent or guardian. *Mick* gives it to anyone who writes to him about a visit to an interesting place, such as a museum, historical building, art gallery, etc. Tell him what you liked best about your visit, and what you learned from it. This badge is also given to anyone who takes up a sport they have never done before, or who introduced a friend to a new sport.

Ten for a Bird You Must Not Miss
You can only be awarded this badge if you actually appear on Magpie.

ANSWERS

PAGE 9

1 9 and 12.

2

3

4

BEGIN   END

5 Neither, a pound weighs a pound whatever it is made of.

7

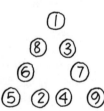

PAGE 65

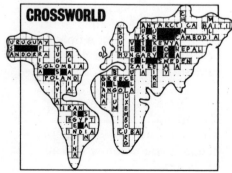

CROSSWORLD

PAGE 97

THE MAGPIE BELONGS TO THE CROW FAMILY. THE COMMON MAGPIE HAS BLACK AND WHITE PLUMAGE AND A LONG TAIL. IT FEEDS ON INSECTS, SNAILS AND MICE AND OFTEN ROBS OTHER BIRDS NESTS OF EGGS AND YOUNG. IT HIDES SURPLUS FOOD AND ALSO ANY COLOURFUL OR SHINY OBJECTS WHICH ATTRACT ITS ATTENTION. IT IS FOUND IN EUROPE, ASIA AND NORTH AFRICA.

PAGE 99

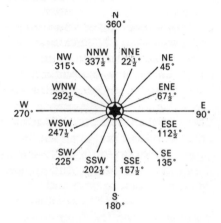

PAGE 100

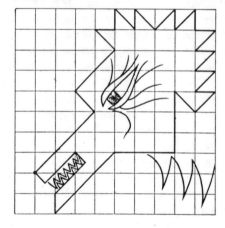

PAGE 102/3

Score one point for each correct answer

1 Bernie Taupin.
2. They have all been winning performers in the Eurovision Song Contest.
3 Guys and Dolls.
4 Eric Clapton.
5 Ian Mitchell.
6 Olivia Newton John.
7 Arrows.
8 Elvis Presley.
9 Leo Sayer.
10 He is a record producer.

11 Buddy Holly.
12 The Supremes.
13 Pete Townshend. The Who.
14 Four Seasons.
15 Chuck Berry.

16 Gary Glitter.
17 Kiki Dee.
18 Elton John.
19 Twiggy.
20 David Bowie.

21 Detroit, Michigan.
22 Isle of Wight.
23 Nashville, Tennessee.
24 Jamaica.
25 Liverpool.

26 Rod Stewart.
27 Stevie Wonder.
28 Paul McCartney.
29 Alice Cooper.
30 Diana Ross.

31 Rod Stewart.
32 David Essex.
33 Freddy Mercury.
34 Lyndsey De Paul.
35 Leslie McKeown.

36 Eight.
37 GBD.
38 Speed.
39 A flat.
40 An interval.

41 New Faces.
42 Mike Batt.
43 'Godspell', 'Jesus Christ Superstar', 'Stardust'.
44 Lyndsey De Paul.
45 'Bugsy Malone.

46 Peter Ilyitch Tschaikowsky.
47 'Amahl and the Night Visitors.'
48 Vienna, Austria.
49 'Silent Night.'
50 Serge Prokofief.

Scoring (maximum possible score 55 points).
45–55: Outstanding. You really are a budding music mastermind.
30–44: Very good. You have a good memory for what you hear.
10–29: Average. You enjoy music, but have a strong preference for some kinds of music over others.
Less than 10: With you, music is something that goes in one ear and out the other. Never mind, you probably have other keen interests.